HOW TO INVEST
IN REAL ESTATE

HOW TO INVEST
IN REAL ESTATE

Maurice A. Unger
Professor of Real Estate
and Business Law
University of Colorado

McGraw-Hill Book Company
New York ● St. Louis ● San Francisco ● Auckland ● Dusseldorf ● Johannesburg
Kuala Lumpur ● London ● Mexico ● Montreal ● New Delhi ● Panama ● Paris
São Paulo ● Singapore ● Sydney ● Tokyo ● Toronto

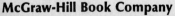

678910111213 FGFG 8321

Library of Congress Cataloging in Publication Data

Unger, Maurice Albert, 1917–
   How to invest in real estate.

   Includes index.
   1. Real estate investment. I. Title.
HD1379.U53   332.6'324   75-23303
ISBN 0-07-065915-X

Contents

1 / WHY REAL ESTATE?

The purpose of this book is to present the basic concepts of real estate investing. It is hoped that the information provided here will enable a person to understand the sometimes "private" jargon of the real estate investor. In addition to focusing on the reasons for investing in real estate, the book explains property selection and taxation, real estate financing, and investment analysis, but first. . .

What is real estate?

Real estate is the land and everything that is erected on, growing upon, or affixed to it; crops requiring annual cultivation are not included in this definition.

What's so hot about real estate investments?

Aside from their relatively high earnings compared with the earnings from other investment opportunities, real estate investments are a super hedge against inflation. In addition, they provide an excellent tax shelter (much about this aspect later, in Chapter 10).

What is inflation?

The simplest way to think of inflation is as a persistent rise in the prices of goods and services. This means that the dollar buys less and less during an inflationary period, as every shopper is now acutely aware. The dime phone call is now fifteen cents in some parts of the nation, and the nickel candy bar has achieved the dubious distinction of an extinct species.

What are the end results of inflation?

Usually inflation is devastating for the individual. For example, you lend a man $1,000 today and he agrees to pay you back a year from now. Suppose prices double during that year. Then you will be repaid, in terms of *real purchasing power*, only about half as much as you loaned.

People living on fixed incomes, such as retirees, finding themselves because of inflated prices faced with bills they cannot pay, must then reduce their standard of living.

Isn't that exaggerating a bit?

Maybe, but not very much. A United States government savings bond for which an individual paid $75 in 1965 returned $100 in 1975. But the $100 received in 1975 bought less in goods and services than could be bought for $72 in 1965.

In other words, instead of making any money, the investor in savings bonds actually lost more than $3 after a 10-year wait. Adding insult to injury, the long arm of the Internal

Revenue Service reached out and taxed the investor on $25 that was *never* received in purchasing power.

Inflation is truly the modern-day terror—it's worse than anything an imagination could dream up. Inflation compounds. The Social Security Administration, fooling around with statistics, assumed a rate of inflation of 2 3/4 percent per year. The 1974 rate was nearly 12 percent, and 1975's may be worse. The Administration also assumed a modest annual pay hike of 5 percent per year and then reached the startling conclusion that people now in their twenties due to retire around the year 2015 will receive $3,000 per month in social security payments if they are married. *But* as a result of the 2 3/4 percent yearly inflation, the $3,000 would be worth only $981 in today's dollars. And realistically, *at the current rate of inflation, $3,000 per month will buy less than 20 percent of $981 in 2015.*

When will inflation stop?

Probably never. The best hope is for a slowdown to a modest 3 percent annually. The energy shortage is a key factor. So long as there is a need to import oil, there will be constant upward pressure on the prices of goods and services. Rising oil costs mean rising costs of plastics, drugs, synthetics, and farm products. Furthermore, transportation costs have increased due to the rise in oil price, and there has been a concomitant rise in the cost of food and other products.

How is inflation measured?

The most common barometer of inflation is the Consumer Price Index. Technically the CPI is entitled the "Index of Change in the Price of Goods and Services Purchased by

Urban Wage-Earners and Clerical-Worker Families to Maintain Their Level of Living." What it amounts to is an index of the prices of 400 goods and services gathered in 56 cities.

It is said to be a *barometer* of inflation because if an individual's income fails to keep up with a rise in the index, then that individual is falling behind in terms of what his or her money will buy. For example, if the index rises 20 percent and your income remains the same, you will lose somewhat less than 20 percent in purchasing power.[1]

What's all this got to do with real estate investments?

Simply that the prices of all the goods and services in the CPI *do not* inflate at the same rate. The change in the cost of electricity versus the change in the cost of steel is a good example.

What this adds up to is the fact that there is *general* inflation, reflected in the Consumer Price Index, and *specific* inflation. Specific inflation is the price rise of a particular item among the 400 goods and services making up the

---

[1] Your loss in purchasing power is less than 20 percent because when prices rise the dollar falls in value, but not by as much as prices rise. Thus if prices go up 100 percent, the value of your dollar cannot fall 100 percent to zero. It is still worth something. The formula is:

$$\frac{\text{Base year prices (currently 1967)}}{\text{Prices this year}} = \frac{\text{Value of dollars in current year}}{\text{Value of money in base year}}$$

Thus

$$\frac{100}{120} = \frac{X}{100} \text{ of } 120\,X = 10,000 \text{ or } X = 83.33$$

Then

$$100 - 83.33 = 16.67\% \text{ decline of dollar value}$$

Consumer Price Index. The most spectacular rise among these particular items occurs in the price of real estate (including rents).

For example, between 1970 and 1971 the Consumer Price Index rose 4.61 percent (currently it is rising about 8 percent yearly). Between 1970 and 1971 construction costs (a particular item) based on an average of 30 United States cities rose a whopping 14.53 percent. This means that you, the average consumer, lost nearly 4.61 percent of the purchasing power of the dollar. More important, persons holding real estate, including private residences, gained nearly 14.53 percent in the value of their real property holdings. Thus persons holding real estate *gained* from inflation— they experienced a *net gain* of 9.92 percent (14.53% − 4.61% = 9.92%).

Not only were holders of real estate protected against inflation, but also inflation caused them to make a profit. Why? Because real estate inflates at a *faster* rate than does the cost of living.

And inflation continues. Between January 1973 and March of that same year, a mere three months, the rise in cost of lumber alone caused the price of the *average* American home to jump $1,200.

Are there any risks in real estate investing?

All investments have risks, some more so than others. In general, there are four types of investment risks; some investments have all four, some three, and so on.

What are the four investment risks?

1 *The Purchasing-Power Risk* Inflation is a purchasing-power risk. Income from an investment can be wiped out

easily by inflation or loss of purchasing power. Furthermore, Uncle Sam the Tax Man hovers over your shoulder impatiently awaiting his cut.

Suppose, for example, that you've put your hard-earned savings into a safe, insured savings account. You've been handed a warm, cuddly blanket as a gift, and you will be paid 5.25 percent interest on the deposit. Inflation is at the rate of, say, 4.5 percent. At the end of the year, then, your bank interest amounts to a net gain of only 0.75 percent (5.25% − 4.50% = 0.75%). This is sorry enough, but the IRS, conveniently forgetting about inflation, slaps a tax on the entire 5.25 percent interest paid to you by the institution. After paying the tax and counting not only the loss of purchasing power on the interest you've earned but also the loss in value of your deposit, you've got to come up a net loser. Maybe not quite—presumably you've still got the cuddly blanket.

2 *The Earning-Power Risk or Risk of Business Failure*
The market risk comes about as a result of fluctuation in the market price of securities over time. This fluctuation can result from many causes. As an investor your control over it is nearly zero.

For instance, you own stock in an auto manufacturer of large, gas-eating luxury cars. Along comes the energy crunch, and automobile sales decline 50 percent. You've had it through no fault of your own.

Suppose that a firm in which you've invested decides to become a conglomerate. Hungrily it gobbles up other firms. Too late, ill-informed, management discovers its inability to digest them. Corporate heartburn, indigestion, and general malaise take over. The conglomerate's holdings are regurgitated one by one. Earnings fall, the price of your stock plunges, and you are left with painful scars.

Even fraud appears to be playing a prominent part in controlling the price of stocks these days. Equity Funding was until a few years ago the stock market's darling, until someone got caught with a hand in the cookie jar. All this incident proved was that the computer can be taught to cheat—with the unwary and innocent investor left holding the bag . . . again. Again.

3 *The Interest-Rate Risk* The interest-rate risk is particularly high in investments in bonds and preferred stocks. You as an individual investor have absolutely no control whatsoever over this. *None.*

When the rate of interest changes, the price of your securities fluctuates even if you're holding United States government bonds or other securities put out by federal, state, or local governments.

Changes in interest rates are typically brought about by the Federal Reserve Board, the big city banks, or both.

The basic and fundamental rules of financial life are as follows:

Rule One: *As interest rates rise, prices of existing bonds and mortgages fall.*

Rule Two: *Conversely, when interest rates fall, prices of existing bonds and mortgages rise.*

Memorize them, think about them, and heed them.

There's nothing magical about these facts of financial life. Actually they make a great deal of sense. Suppose you bought an AAA-rated bond four years ago for $1,000 at 6 percent interest. Your ownership of the bond means that the firm to whom you loaned the money has a contractual obligation to pay you $60 interest annually and to return your $1,000 on the maturity date of the bond.

Okay, you hold the bond for four years. Assume that suddenly the interest rate rises to 12 percent. This means that if another corporation decides to float a bond issue now, it has to agree to pay new purchasers of each $1,000 bond $120 per year.

You say to yourself, "The smart thing to do is to sell my old bond paying $60 per year and take the money and buy a new one that will pay $120." Unhappily you'll soon discover that most of the other holders of the lower-interest bonds are thinking the same thing, and they, too, are starting to dump their bonds. Theoretically, depending on the maturity date, the market price of your bond will fall to $500. Why? Because whoever buys it will demand a 12 percent return or the current market rate, and your bond pays only 6 percent per year, or $60. However at a price of $500 it will be earning for its new owner 12 percent interest or the current market rate ($500 × 12% = $60).

In real life the price decline depends on how far in the future the bond matures. Obviously if the bond is due in six months the price won't fall to $500. It most certainly won't fall that far, because you and the other bondholders are aware that if you hold your bonds for six months more your $1,000 will be repaid. And you'd be wise to wait. However, if you do want to cash out today, the bond price will fall somewhat. Thus, with rising interest rates, existing bond prices inevitably fall.

Suppose, however, that interest rates decline, say to 3 percent. What will happen to the market price of the old bond paying 6 percent, or $60 per year? All a new investor can expect with the 3 percent rate is $30 a year on each $1,000 invested. As a result, the investor will begin shopping around for a higher return on his or her money.

What will happen then? Demand will increase for the old bonds paying 6 percent. With increased demand, market prices are forced up. Theoretically, again depending on the maturity date of the old bond, the price will rise to $2,000. This means that the buyer of the old bond will still receive only a 3 percent yield ($2,000 × 3% = $60). The $60, of course, is the contractual rate of the old bond. In the real world of business the price will never go that high, but it *will* go up. Thus, with declining interest rates, bond prices rise.

Even supposedly astute bankers are not immune to the risk of interest-rate changes. One of the many reasons given for the financial debacle downing Long Island's Franklin National Bank in 1974 was its bond-purchasing policy. The bank bought bonds at a time when interest rates were on the rise. As a result, the market price of the bonds fell; the bank's portfolio was left frozen, thus contributing to the bank's nonliquidity.

The fourth investment risk will be discussed on page 11, but first. . .

What causes changes in interest rates?

Changes in interest rates are not too difficult to understand if money is thought of as being like any other commodity, say dried beans. If the supply of beans is high, then it follows that the price will fall (provided demand remains the same). If the supply of beans is low, the price of beans will rise (provided demand remains the same).

The same thing happens with money. Supply high–price falls. Supply low–price rises. *Interest is the price we pay for money.*

Who controls the supply of money? For the most part it is controlled by the Federal Reserve Board.

What is the Federal Reserve Board?

The Federal Reserve Board is more accurately referred to as "the Board of Governors of the Federal Reserve System." The Board consists of seven persons appointed for 14 years. It was created by the Federal Reserve Act passed by Congress in 1913.

The act divided the country up into 12 Federal Reserve Districts with a Federal Reserve Bank in each district. The initial capital was obtained through sale of stock to commercial banks within the districts. The subscribers are called the "member banks." Although the Federal Reserve Banks are owned by member banks, the Federal Reserve Board works closely with the President and the Treasury Department. In reality, it is a central banking authority.

What are the Board's chief headaches?

Mainly its members worry about two economic problems: inflation and deflation (sometimes called a *recession* or *depression*—depending on who's doing the calling).

The Board members may reason, if worrying about inflation, that interest rates should be raised. How? By reducing the supply of money. Why reduce the supply of money and thereby raise interest rates? The Board members feel that if rates are raised, then a business executive will hesitate to borrow at the higher interest rates. What difference does this make? Suppose a new factory was being contemplated; with higher rates the executive most likely won't borrow and consequently won't put inflationary pressures on lumber, steel, wages, and the like.

If, conversely, the Reserve Board fears recession, it tends to lower interest rates. With lower rates, executives will borrow. When money is borrowed and used for new construction, demand for labor and materials will increase, thereby giving the economy a needed shot in the arm.

One of the dilemmas sometimes faced by the Board is that when interest rates are raised, the resulting slowdown in the economy will decrease employment. Further, inflation may not be reduced by much. Board members then find themselves caught in a trade-off between slowing down inflation and causing massive unemployment.

The tools used by the Board to shift the rates are highly technical and need not be dealt with here.

What's the fourth investment risk?

The fourth investment risk is the risk of *nonliquidity*. This means the risk of loss a person runs if forced to turn his assets quickly into cash. Obviously the more liquid an asset, the less need there is for sacrifice when converting to cash. Real estate is the least liquid of all assets; it takes time to sell. But the benefits of investing in real estate are greater than those of any of the other investment opportunities.

The table on the following page shows the risks involved in alternative investment opportunities as well as the historical rates of return on each type.

Investment Evaluation Matrix
assuming 3 percent inflation

Investment Media	Gross Before-Tax Rate of Return, %	Net Before-Tax Rate of Return, %*	Primary Risk Types
Cash	Nonearning asset	−3.0	1 Purchasing power
Savings accounts	4–5¼	1–2¼	1 Purchasing power
Savings Certificates of Deposit	4½–6	1½–3	1 Purchasing power
United States government bonds, notes, and certificates	3–6	0–3	1 Interest rate 2 Purchasing power
Corporate bonds	6½–7½	3½–4½	1 Interest rate 2 Purchasing power 3 Market
Preferred stocks	5–8	2–5	1 Interest rate 2 Market 3 Purchasing power
Common stocks	Historically 9	6	1 Market 2 Earning power 3 Purchasing power
Real estate	Normal range 10–15	7–12	1 Nonliquidity

*Net before-tax rate of return is obtained after deducting an average rate of inflation, for illustration purposes, of 3 percent rounded off.

Source: Karvel, George R. and Donald A. Rogers, *Real Estate and the Competition for Investment Dollars*. Center for Real Estate and Land Use Studies, Business Research Division, Graduate School of Business Administration, University of Colorado, May 1972, p. 6.

2 / REAL ESTATE OWNERSHIP

There are many different forms in which to hold or own real estate. Each form has its own peculiarities in the sense that the legal consequences of each form of ownership are different. Furthermore, the tax savings or tax impact may also differ.

hat are the forms of real estate ownership?

You can own real property as an individual, tenants in common, joint tenants, tenants by the entireties, community property, a partnership, a syndicate, a limited partnership, a corporation, or a shareholder in a real estate investment trust.

ow can a person acquire real property individually?

It's easy. The seller conveys parcels of real property to you by a deed. In 99 out of 100 cases you have a *fee simple es-*

tate. This means absolute ownership. You (it's in your name alone now) record the deed in the office of the Clerk of the County, or in some states it's called "the Recorder's office," in which the property is located. Anytime you wish you may sell the property; it is also transferable by will or by intestacy (without a will) upon death.

The reason this deed and all deeds, for that matter, should be recorded immediately is to give notice to the world that title has passed from the seller or donor to another person. In the absence of recording, the seller can sell the property to someone else. If the other party records first (in the absence of fraud) it's his or hers. The general rule regarding recording is, "First in time, first in right."

Shouldn't something more be said about deeds?

Yes. By definition a *deed* is an instrument in writing which conveys (transfers, if you prefer) an interest in real property. Although standard texts on real estate mention many different kinds of deeds, there are basically only three. The others are variations on a theme. Beginning with the simplest kind of deed and moving to the most complicated, they are

1 *The Quitclaim Deed* This states that the grantor (maker of the deed, either selling the property or just giving it away) transfers to the grantee (recipient) the grantor's rights, *if any*, in the property described. In other words, if I've got good title to the described property, then you get good title. If I haven't got good title, then you get bad title. In short, I give you what I've got, if anything.

2 *The Bargain and Sale Deed* This varies from the quitclaim deed in the following way. If I quitclaim to you, I

say, "I give you what I've got, if anything." But in the bargain and sale deed, I assert by implication that I possess a claim to or an interest in the property. This claim or interest is not present in the quitclaim deed.

3 *The Warranty Deed* A warranty deed is a deed in which the owner of real property warrants that he or she has good and merchantable title to the property being conveyed. The deed contains five covenants: The first covenant is *seizin*—here the grantor states that he or she has full possession of whatever quantum of estate is being conveyed. The second covenant is *quiet enjoyment* —this means that if the grantee is evicted by either the grantor or a third person having better title, then the grantee has a cause of action against the grantor. The third is the *covenant of further assurance*, which means that the grantor agrees to perform acts necessary to perfect title for the grantee. For example, if the description in the original deed is incorrect, the grantor has to correct it. The fourth is the *covenant against encumbrances*—this means that if there are encumbrances against the property not mentioned in the deed, then the covenant is violated and the grantee can sue the grantor. Examples of encumbrances are tax liens, mortgages, etc. The fifth is the *covenant of warranty of title* —here the grantor warrants the title. If a third person has better title, then the grantor is liable for any damages sustained by the grantee.[1]

---

[1] In New York State there is an additional statutory covenant, a *covenant of trust*. It makes the grantor the trustee of funds received from the sale of the property for the benefit of any potential mechanic's lienors. In California a special warranty deed is used: here the grantor warrants only claims asserted by, through, or under him or her.

What is a tenancy in common?

A *tenancy in common* exists when two or more persons own the same land with undivided interests. Frequently investments in real property are made this way. Two or three persons chip in on the down payment. Each tenant in common then reports on his or her income tax the proportionate share of the income and expenses.

If it turns out that one of your co-tenants fails to pay his or her share of the expenses, then you're stuck. In more ways than one. Even if you pay his or her share, you can still deduct only your share of the expenses. Taxwise the rest is considered as an advance to your co-tenant.

A co-tenant's share can be sold or disposed of by will. Meaning that it's possible for you to wind up as a tenant in common with a stranger.

What is a joint tenancy?

A *joint tenancy* exists when two or more persons own the same real property and have the same unity of interest, time, title, and possession together with the right of survivorship. The right of survivorship is the most important feature of the joint tenancy. Frequently it is referred to as "the grand incident" of the joint tenancy.

For example, suppose you, Frances, and Joe own a small investment in real property as joint tenants. Joe dies. This means that the title to the property passes to you and Frances. Implicit in the right of survivorship is the rule of law that the property *cannot* be disposed of by will. Furthermore, the property does not have to go through a probate court, and the survivors hold title to the property free and clear from debts and claims against the deceased joint tenant. In a few states husband and wife are permitted to hold property as joint tenants.

What is a tenancy by the entireties?[2]

A tenancy by the entireties exists generally only in real property and exists only between husband and wife. The deed must be made out to both of them, at the same time, while they are married. The surviving spouse gets title to the entire property upon the death of the other. Neither can sell the property without first obtaining the signature of the other on the deed.

In case of divorce the man and woman become tenants in common without the right of survivorship. The theory behind this law is that under the common law, husband and wife were considered one. After a divorce there is no longer a unity; hence there can be no tenancy by the entireties and there is a tenancy in common.

What is community property?[3]

Community property is a joint interest held between husband and wife. In general, real property acquired by either the husband or wife during marriage is held jointly, provided that it is not the separate property of either spouse. Property owned by each before the marriage is considered separate property. The surviving spouse automatically gets one-half of the community property. The remaining

---

[2]This form is recognized in the states of Arkansas, Delaware, Florida, Indiana, Kentucky, Maryland, Massachusetts, Michigan, Missouri, New Jersey, New York, North Carolina, Oklahoma, Oregon, Pennsylvania, Rhode Island, Tennessee, Vermont, West Virginia, Wisconsin, and Wyoming.

[3]Community property exists in Arizona, California, Idaho, Nevada, New Mexico, Louisiana, Texas, and Washington.

half can be disposed of by will to anyone to whom the person making the will wants it to go.

What is partnership property?

In simple terms, *partnership property* is real property to which title is held in the name of a partnership. Thus if John Smith and Jane Doe hold partnership realty and Jane dies, the title to the partnership property rests in the surviving partner. *But* the surviving partner must manage the property properly and move to terminate the partnership. The survivor has to account to the estate of the deceased partner. Unlike in the joint tenancy, the heirs of the deceased partner are not automatically cut off.

Like in any partnership, ordinarily the act of one partner binds the others. However, in the case of partnership realty, all the partners must sign a deed in order to transfer the property. *Unless* one partner has specific authorization (a power of attorney signed by the other partner or partners, and recorded) to sign the deed.

What is syndicate property?

Simply defined, a *syndicate* is a joint venture involving two or more persons. It's used when several persons chip in for the purpose of buying real property. Five or six persons can throw in as little as $1,000 each. Typically there is a syndicate agreement including a statement reciting the amount contributed by each member and the way the money is to be disposed of in case of the death of any member, and a statement concerning the property purchased or about to be purchased. Sometimes a syndicate manager is appointed. More often than not the manager is a Realtor who is given control over matters pertaining to the purchase and management of the property.

The tax shelter is available to the syndicate members on

a pro rata basis, making it like individual ownership of income-producing property. Furthermore, syndicate members may take advantage of long-term capital gains tax deductions if the opportunity arises.

The chief things distinguishing the syndicate from the limited partnership are the number of members and, often, the total amount to be invested.

hat is a limited partnership?

A *limited partnership* consists of a general partner and a number of limited partners. The limited partners put up the cash; they are the equity investors. With the money the general partner buys and/or develops a parcel of real property, say, a luxury motel. The property is managed by the general partner for a fee. The limited partners have no say whatsoever in how the partnership is run, except in the case of fraud on the part of the general partner.

The liability of the limited partners is *limited* to the amount of their contribution to the partnership capital. If the deal sours, it's up to the general partner to handle the creditors. The partnership terminates with the death of the general partner, but it does not end with the death of any of the limited partners; a limited partner's shares, or *units*, as they are often called, pass to his or her heirs.

ow do limited partnerships really work?

Like so! Suppose a builder-developer gets an option on a parcel of commercially zoned land. To promote the land the developer decides to form a limited partnership. Units are then sold to individuals, with the promoter as the general partner and the individuals as limited partners. The limited-partnership shares are generally priced out at anywhere from $1,000 up. You may buy as many as you like.

Often the deal provides that the general partner, in return for acting as such, is to get 5 percent (or more) of the action plus as high as 50 percent (or whatever the promoter of the partnership figures the traffic will bear) of any capital appreciation realized upon the sale of the property after the limited partners get back their capital investment.

More often than not, the payments made by the limited partners are made in installments, for example, so much down and so much periodically until the project is completed.

Why are limited partnerships so popular?

There are two main reasons. One is that a limited partnership is a tax shelter. Unlike expenses of the corporation, partnership expenses "pass through" pro rata to the limited partners. As such the expenses are deductible on the partners' individual tax returns. Furthermore, any "depreciation" also passes through and may be deducted by a limited partner. In the event that the property is sold and there is some capital appreciation, the gain may be subject to the long-term capital gains tax. (Capital gains will be detailed in the chapter on taxation.)

A second reason for the popularity of the limited partnership is that it may enable you to take advantage of a real estate investment with a relatively small amount of cash. The fact of the matter is that the cost of shares or units in current limited partnerships averages about $5,000 each. But there's nothing to prevent you and a couple of your friends from chipping in on a $5,000 unit.

Are there any special risks in a limited partnership?

There are many risks. First, the general partner may be a bit overzealous and project future incomes unreasonably high. For example, if the project is a luxury apartment building, rental income could be estimated much higher than should be reasonably expected considering the location of the project. The project may be located in the wrong place simply because prospective tenants in that area may not have sufficient income to support a luxury apartment project.

The second, and probably the greatest, risk is the exceedingly high degree of nonliquidity of limited-partnership units. No organized market exists. If you are forced to sell your units, you are almost 100 percent certain to suffer a loss.

Are limited partnerships regulated?

Yes, in several ways. If the limited partnership is a *public* offering rather than a *private* one, then the offering must be registered with the Securities and Exchange Commission. This means, among other things, that prospective buyers must be given a prospectus which contains a full disclosure of all the facts, circumstances, and risks involved in the investment.

What are public and private offerings?

Most people consider a private offering to be one to 25 or fewer persons. An offering to more than 25 persons is considered a public offering.

Oddly enough, the term *private offering* has never been statutorily defined. Furthermore, some states have their own definitions. Some define it as an offering to 10 or fewer persons. For all practical purposes, limited-partnership offerings must be registered with the Securities and Exchange Commission.

This being so, they are regarded as securities and must be sold through licensed dealers. This means that if a limited partnership is offered for sale by a real estate broker, the broker must have passed the security license exam of the state in which the sale is consummated.

How about a corporation organized to hold real estate?

Chief Justice Marshall defined a corporation as "an artificial being, indivisible, intangible, and a device only in contemplation of law." However, a modern-day wag may have defined it a bit better: "A corporation is an artificial person with no soul to be damned and no ass to be kicked."

A corporation is an entity separate and distinct from its shareholders. The shareholders who own the corporation are not liable for the debts of the corporation. The shareholders are said to have *limited liability* for the corporate debts. All that creditors can seize are the assets actually owned by the corporation. In other words, if you are a shareholder in a corporation and it goes belly up, creditors cannot grab your personal assets.

Generally speaking, the typical corporation formed especially for investing in real estate is probably bad news. The main reason is *double taxation*. This means that the corporation (the separate entity) is taxed on its earnings, and when the corporation distributes profits to the owners (to you as one of the stockholders), these monies are then taxed for the second time.

Note: Some closely held corporations can elect to be taxed as partnerships. In this case the double tax is avoided. The owners pay taxes on earnings as if they were partners. The shareholders, if they do elect to be taxed as a partnership, can deduct their expenses from income obtained from other sources.

Corporations of this type are *Subchapter S corporations* (from Subchapter S of the Internal Revenue Code). To qualify, the corporation must be a "small business corporation." This is defined as a corporation having not more than 10 shareholders, who must be individuals or estates. The shareholders cannot be another corporation nor can they be nonresident aliens.

All shareholders must consent to tax treatment under Subchapter S. *But* if more than 20 percent of the corporation's *gross receipts* (not gross income or net income) is passive investment income, tax treatment under Subchapter S terminates. *Passive investment income* is gross receipts from annuities, dividends, interest, royalties, and rents.

This means you've got to be careful, especially when your income is from rents, because having this type of income will normally violate the passive investment income rule. If it does then the corporation will be taxed like any other corporation, and in addition, shareholders will be taxed on any income received from the corporation.

What is a real estate investment trust?

Congress set up the real estate investment trust, or REIT, as it is called, effective January 1, 1961. The purpose was to afford the "little man" a tax shelter and an opportunity to invest in real estate to a limited degree.

The tax shelter comes about because the REIT is *not* treated as a corporation for tax purposes. Only the income to the individual is taxed. There is no double taxation as in the ordinary corporation, where the corporate income is taxed first and income to the investor (stockholder) is taxed again.

How are REITs organized?

Basically as follows:

1 The shares that are bought through a stockbroker must be held by 100 or more beneficial owners.

2 The shares must be freely transferable.

3 One or more trustees must manage a REIT.

4 A REIT must elect with the Internal Revenue Service to be treated as a real estate investment trust.

5 It must not hold property primarily for sale to customers in the ordinary course of business. In other words, it can't just buy and sell real estate.

6 At least 90 percent of gross income must be derived from dividends, interest, rents on real property, or gains from real estate securities. The last means mortgages.

7 Seventy-five percent of gross income must be derived from rents, interest on mortgages, or real property interests. This is to prevent wheeling and dealing in real estate mortgages.

8 And less than 30 percent of gross income may be from the sale or other disposition of stock or securities held for less than six months and real property held for less than four years. Again, this prevents any wheeling and dealing in real property itself.

What kinds of REITs are there?

There are three types of REITs.

1 *Equity Trusts* These trusts invest equity capital in real estate projects, hoping for rental income. For example, a

REIT might be organized to put together and own a shopping center.

2 *Mortgage Trusts* In this case, REITs finance projects. For example, some REITs specialize, to a degree, in financing motels. They lend the money and receive income in the form of interest.

3 *A Combination of the Above Two Types* This is the most common. Some money goes into equities and some into loans.

ow do REITs stack up as investments?

Well, they are stocks and are sold in the stock market, and today's darling is frequently tomorrow's bum. During a period of high interest rates, overbuilding, and material shortages, the REIT finds the going tough. For example, in 1975, under these conditions, a number of REITs filed bankruptcy petitions. What's worse: under certain conditions, the shareholders of a REIT *can be assessed* for certain debts of an insolvent trust. This means that you, the shareholder, can have your personal assets seized by creditors, given the proper circumstances.

3 / METHODS AND INSTRUMENTS OF FINANCING

Financing is the heart of most real estate transactions. "No financing, no transaction" is the general rule. The reason, of course, is the relatively large amounts of money involved. Because they require so much money, most real estate transactions involve loans with the real property used as the collateral for the loan. Thus the prospective real estate investor has to have a working knowledge of both the methods of financing and the legal instruments protecting the lenders as well as the investors.

How are real estate investments financed?

Moving from the simplest to the more complicated, there are basically five methods: paying cash; assuming an existing mortgage or deed of trust; making a contract for deed (same as an installment land contract); arranging a purchase-money mortgage; or starting from scratch, namely, borrowing from a financial institution. Cash is rarely used for a number of reasons, as will be pointed out later.

What is assuming a mortgage or existing deed of trust?[1]

First of all, a mortgage is a lien against a parcel of real property. In short, you borrow money and promise to pay; and the land is used as the collateral. A deed of trust (in the nature of a mortgage) works the same way, with a minor exception. The borrower transfers title to the property to a trustee for the benefit of the lender. If the borrower fails to pay, the trustee forecloses for the lender. For all practical purposes, a deed of trust is used because the foreclosure action can be completed more rapidly.

Now, back to the original question. Assuming a mortgage or deed of trust works like this. Suppose you spot a $50,000 investment property with an existing mortgage of $40,000. You can pay the seller $10,000 in cash and assume the $40,000 mortgage. In short, you have promised to pay that amount to the lender in the same manner that the borrower has been doing. In return, the property is deeded over to you.

What's a contract for deed?

A contract for deed is one way a seller can finance the sale of property. It's used in many sales of vacant land and oddly enough extensively in the sale of farms and ranches.

---

[1]The deed of trust is used in California, Colorado, Delaware, the District of Columbia, Illinois, Mississippi, Nevada, New Mexico, Tennessee, Texas, Utah, Virginia, and West Virginia. In Montana it can be used only on parcels of 3 acres or less.

Say you want to speculate on vacant land. It's almost 100 percent impossible at this stage of the game to obtain a loan from a financial institution. So you and the seller enter into a contract; you give the seller the cash down and agree to pay the balance monthly, yearly, or whatever. You get delivery of the deed after you've paid off the seller.

At the signing of the contract, however, the seller has the deed prepared and signs it. Then the deed, along with a copy of the contract, is delivered to a third person (called an *escrow agent*), whose instructions are to deliver the deed after you've paid off the contract. Generally you make your payments to the escrow agent, who transmits the funds to the seller after taking out a small fee for services.

The reason the deed is given to an escrow agent is that the seller might die before the contract is paid off, and you would have to hassle with the executor of the estate to get the deed. Besides, suppose the seller was married when you signed the contract and divorced at the time you finished paying? You'd pay hell chasing after the ex-spouse to obtain a signature on the deed.

Warning One: If you ever buy land or other real property "on contract," make certain that the contract is in recordable form. That is, it must be signed by all parties in the presence of a notary public; then you should record it in the office of the Clerk of the County in which the property is located. This recording gives notice to the world that you are buying the property. Then if your seller tries to sell the same piece of land to someone else after your contract is recorded, the other buyer will get burned, not you. Again: the rule is, "First in time, first in right." Yes, there *really* are crooks in the world.

Warning Two: The contract will contain a nasty little clause in very small type which may burn the buyer badly. It will say, in effect, that if the buyer misses a payment, the down payment and all others that may have been made are forfeited to the seller as liquidated damages, and the seller has a right to come upon the property and get it back free and clear. The seller must, however, give the buyer notice of the forfeiture; in most states, the buyer then has 60 to 90 days to come up with the entire balance due.

Sometimes the courts won't entirely buy this nasty clause, but nobody really knows at what point they won't. To exaggerate a bit, suppose you're buying a $100,000 piece of property on contract. You've made all your payments except for the last $1,000. The seller yells, "Gotcha! You forfeit $99,000 and I get the property back."

In this case the courts would probably make the seller put the property up for auction at a public sale. The seller would get the first $1,000 obtained at the sale and you, the buyer, all the money over that amount. But no one knows at precisely what point the courts would force a seller to auction off a property, sell it, or just give it to the buyer.

Moral: Try, if possible, to avoid the contract for deed. Suggest the purchase-money mortgage. If you use a purchase-money mortgage and then are unable to make payments, the seller must foreclose and put the property up for public sale. In this case any surplus amount bid over the indebtedness automatically goes to you.

What's a purchase-money mortgage?

A purchase-money mortgage is when the seller *takes back* a mortgage as part of the purchase price. Suppose the seller owns a piece of property free and clear and wants

$60,000 for it. You give the seller $10,000 down and he or she gives you a deed and takes back a mortgage for $50,000. All future payments are then made directly to the seller.

Why should a seller do that? Why shouldn't the seller send you to a financial institution to obtain a loan? First, you may not be able to get a loan from an institution with only $10,000 down. Second, it may be a good deal for the seller in the sense that you'll have to pay interest on the balance. The seller probably can get upwards of 8 percent interest from you, which is better than getting 6 percent on a Certificate of Deposit in a savings and loan association.

Warning: In buying real property either on a contract for deed or with a purchase-money mortgage, one thing the buyer should beware of is the *balloon payment*. This can be a disastrous financial trap. What is it? It works like this. Suppose I sell you a piece of property on which $10,000 is to be paid off in five years. We can set up the deal so that you pay me $1,000 per year plus interest for four years, and then in the fifth year the $6,000 balance plus interest comes due. You may be able to get up the $1,000 plus per year easily enough for the first four years, but in the fifth year the *balloon* is going to be $6,000 plus interest. You've got to be damned sure that you're either going to have that sum or can borrow the money when it's due; otherwise you stand a good chance of losing the whole bundle.

ren't options used to finance property?

Sometimes, but often options are used in connection with other financing devices. But first, an option by definition is a contract to keep an offer open. A fundamental rule of contract law is that an offer can be withdrawn at any time before it is accepted. For example, I offer to sell you my antique watch for $500. At any time before you have accepted the offer, I can withdraw it even if I have said you have until next January 20 to accept. But suppose I offer to sell you the watch for $500 and give you the option to accept at any time prior to next January 20 if you pay me $5, then we have an option contract provided you accept the contract and pay me the $5. Under these circumstances I *cannot* withdraw the offer. Why? Because all the elements of the contract are present. We have an offer, a communication of the offer, an acceptance of the offer, and consideration (the $5).

Now let's look at the real estate option. To begin with, *all contracts for the sale of real property must be in writing.* This goes for the real estate option. Typically the real estate option works this way. You own a piece of property and you're asking $10,000 for it. I come to you and say I will give you $500 for six months' option. You agree. (This means that you're taking the property off the market for six months.) Once you give me the option, if I come up with the money in six months or less, you've got to sell the property to me for $10,000. Generally this sort of option is written in one of two ways: if I exercise the option, my $500 is credited toward the purchase price (this means I have to get up only $9,500); or you get to keep the $500 (this means I have to get up the whole $10,000).

Why would anyone want an option?

Simple. Suppose I think you've underpriced the property at $10,000. I think I can get $15,000 for it. The option gives me six months to find another buyer at $15,000. If I find one, I assign the option to him or her. The new buyer gives me $5,000 in cash, exercises the option, and pays you your $10,000. You give the assignee of the option a deed. I net $4,500 ($5,000 less the $500 I paid you). Everyone's happy except you. You kick yourself for under-pricing the property.

Another reason I might want to option is this. I want to subdivide the property, and I'm not sure I can get the financing. The option gives me six months to shop around for money. If I can't get it, all I lose is what I've paid for the option, and I'm not stuck with a piece of land that I might not be able to use.

How is the option often used as a financing gimmick?

It is frequently used by small builders. Suppose you have seven lots which you have priced at $1,000 each, totaling $7,000. Say I'm a small builder (small mostly because I'm short of capital). We can make a deal. I give you $1,000 and you deed me one lot. You give me an option on the other six lots. The agreement can be made so that after I build the first house, you will, upon receiving, say, $500, deed me two additional lots and take back a purchase-money mortgage in the amount of $1,500. When I get up the $1,500, you will release the two lots free and clear of the mortgage. Thus I build the first house, sell it, pay you $1,500 out of profit, and get the other two lots released, and so on.

The advantage to me is that if I fail to make it with the first house or even the second and the third, I simply don't exercise my option.

Unfortunately, in the real world things are not always that simple. As a practical matter, the seller may feel that there is a possibility of getting stuck with some of the lots. And because the seller is taking a risk, he or she may raise the price of each lot, in this case to, say, $1,200. In the end it generally boils down to a matter of price negotiating between the seller and buyer.

How does one go about financing real estate from scratch?

There are basically two situations you may find yourself in. The first situation involves an existing building. Suppose you decide to buy an older apartment house (or any other commercial property, for that matter) for $100,000. The first step is the *contract for the sale of real property* entered into by you and your seller. There are at least two important *contingency clauses* of which you should be acutely aware. Aware, because unhappily they are sometimes overlooked.

Assume the deal is that you are to put $25,000 down and try to obtain a loan from a financial institution for the balance of $75,000. In this case the contract must have a contingency clause reading, in effect, "subject to the buyer obtaining a first mortgage in the amount of $75,000." This clause means that if you've made a reasonable effort to obtain the loan and are unable to do so, then the deal is off, and you're entitled to the return of your down payment (earnest money). In the absence of this clause, you could lose the deposit or find yourself mired in an expensive and time-consuming lawsuit.

Another clause, all too often omitted, is also important in the purchase of any type of income-producing property. This clause has to do with the damage or security deposits in the hands of your seller as well as with the current status of the existing leases the seller has with the tenants. For example, if your seller has $500 of tenants' damage deposits, the contract must provide that this money be turned over to you at the closing. After all, once the property is yours you are responsible for returning the deposit to the tenants if they leave the place undamaged.

Furthermore, suppose the seller tells you that all the leases have three, four, or whatever years to run. Make him or her put this in writing with the proviso that you have the option to void the contract if the leases are not as the seller said they were.

Let's assume that all this has been taken care of and you apply for a loan to a financial institution. But first . . .

What are the financial institutions?

More specifically, the question should be, "What are the financial institutions active in making real estate loans?" The leading mortgage lenders are savings and loan associations, mutual savings banks (located for the most part in the eastern part of the United States), life insurance companies, and, often for larger loans, REITs. One thing to keep in mind, especially during periods of easing or lowering interest rates, is the following: you can shop around for money. This means that you ought to go from one institution to another to see where you can get the best deal.

What happens when you apply for a loan?

First you have to submit a balance sheet. The balance sheet lists your assets, liabilities, and net worth. In addition, you submit what amounts to a personal income and expense statement. The institution has a credit report run on you, and if everything is okay you get the loan and the deal is closed.

Suppose you are going to have a brand-new building built?

This is the second situation referred to under financing real estate. Assume again that the deal is for $100,000, with $25,000 cash down and a loan of $75,000. You sign a contract with a builder. (Actually you sniff around and make damned sure you are going to get the financing first.)

Because the building is going to be built from scratch, there's naturally going to be a lapse between the time the builder starts and the completion date. Say you sign the agreement on March 1 in which the builder agrees to have the structure completed by October 15. First, try to have a penalty clause inserted in the contract. Under this clause the builder has to pay you a stipulated sum for each and every day after the 15th of October that the building is not completed. *But* there's an even more important matter to be inserted in the contract, which we'll see in a moment.

So you've signed the contract with the builder, and you apply to your chosen financial institution for $75,000. It's almost 100 percent certain that you'll have to pay the institution *points* (cash on the barrelhead) as a percentage of the loan. If you want $75,000 and the lender demands one point with your application, you pay $750—for two points you pay $1,500, and so on.

Historically, the financial institutions argued that getting points was really a way for them to recover the cost of setting up the loan. No longer so (if it ever really was)—it's just the cost of getting money, a commitment fee or front end money if you like.

Having received whatever percentage it required, the institution gives you a letter saying that (1) it will lend you the $75,000 on the property on October 15 (the completion date), (2) you will have to pay a stated rate of interest, say, 8 percent, on the loan, and probably (3) you will have to pay more points at the closing. Assume you have to pay one point—another $750.

Things go neatly, the builder builds, and on October 15 you close the deal, take possession of the property, and are on your way.

But—things do not always go smoothly. As a matter of fact, smoothness seems to be the exception rather than the rule. What if your builder *fails* to complete by October 15? You may have had it. With luck, you've got the penalty clause in the builder's contract, so he or she has to come up with a few bucks. But what about your friendly financial institution? After all, the loan commitment was made only until October 15. The financial institution has many choices: It can keep your $750 (points paid on March 1) and tell you to take a walk. It can say, "We like you, friend, so we'll make a new commitment and extend your closing date, but you've got to pay another commitment fee." It can extend the time for free, which is sometimes done. Or *what's worse*—the institution can say, "Okay, friend, we'll extend the loan commitment, *but* since March 1 interest rates have gone up from 8 percent to 9 percent; sorry we're forced to charge you that." Believe it, this extra 1 percent in interest adds up to many dollars over the life of a typical 20-year loan.

What can you do about it?

One thing you can do is to insist on a clause in your contract with the builder to the effect that he or she will pay (1) any extra commitment fees you may suffer as a result of the builder's delay and (2) any extra interest payments that you may suffer as the result of his or her failure to complete the project on time.

What about a second mortgage?

First of all, a *second mortgage* (or deed of trust) is a junior lien against real property. In the final analysis it is "second" because it is recorded after the first mortgage. Generally it carries a higher interest rate and the payoff is in a relatively short period of time.

How are second mortgages used?

Mostly like so. Suppose again that you are interested in buying a $100,000 property. You need $25,000 down, but you have only $15,000—consequently you're short $10,000. You might obtain a loan of $75,000 from a financial institution (which will hold the first mortgage), give the seller the $15,000 cash, and have the seller take back a second purchase-money mortgage in the amount of $10,000.

More often than not, financial institutions won't finance the deal if there's going to be a second mortgage in the picture. Consequently a second mortgage is more commonly used when a mortgage is assumed. For example, suppose that the total price is $100,000, your seller owes the financial institution $70,000, and all you've got is $15,000 in cash, so you are short $15,000. You could work out a deal to give the seller the $15,000 cash, assume the $70,000 mortgage, and have the seller take back a second purchase-money mortgage in the amount of $15,000.

Another angle frequently used is this. Again, assume a purchase price of $100,000 with an existing mortgage of $70,000 and that you have only $15,000 cash. You can give the seller the $15,000, assume the $70,000 mortgage, and go to an individual who will lend you the necessary $15,000 on a second mortgage.

As an alternative to individuals, there is one institution permitted to lend on second mortgages, and this is the industrial bank. But be careful. Industrial banks charge through the nose (as high as 18.5 percent interest), and if things go a bit sour you can be badly burned.

What is a participation?

Something to be avoided wherever possible. What a *participation* amounts to is lenders (either first or second mortgagees) having a piece of the action. Participations can be very messy and very dangerous to the borrower. They come about mostly in periods of high interest rates. For example, you come to me to borrow $100,000. I can play the participation game in many forms and with numerous variations. I can say, "Okay, you can have the $100,000 loan *but* I get a percentage of your gross rents." I might, repeat *might*, give you an interest rate on your loan slightly lower than the going market rate, or I might extend the term of the loan, which means simply that your monthly payments would be lower.

In another variation of the participation I could say, "Okay, I'll lend you the $100,000, *but* if you sell the property, I get 25 percent, 50 percent, or whatever the traffic will bear out of your capital appreciation." In other words, if you sell it for $50,000 over what you paid for it, I wind up with $25,000 of your profit from the transaction.

Still another variation of the participation is, "Okay, I'll lend you the $100,000, *but* I get a percentage of your gross rents *plus* a percentage of any capital appreciation you might have when you sell the property."

What a participation amounts to is the lender having a share in your gains without having to put up any of the equity funds. The lender has virtually no risk of loss. Could be that as a result of his or her participation in your gross rents, you might not make your payments. No sweat as far as the lender's concerned. The lender forecloses, winds up with the property, and leaves you out in the cold.

Moral: Avoid participations like the plague except when absolutely necessary.

4 / THE USE OF LEVERAGE

Leverage is simply using borrowed money to increase gains. It is the key to almost all investment in real property and is based on the assumption that the borrower can earn more in income from borrowed money than what he or she pays to actually borrow the money. Easy enough in principle, and wonderful—if it works.

The idea is this: I borrow from you at, say, 5 percent, turn around and lend the same money out at 6 percent, so I make 1 percent. The rub comes when I don't quite make it. For example, I borrow at 5 percent and can earn only 4 percent—I lose 1 percent.

How does leverage apply to real estate investment?

Almost every parcel sold for investment pruposes is levered in one way or another. The investor uses other people's money.

How does leverage work?

Suppose you have $10,000 to invest in real estate and you can make 10 percent on it. You will have an income of $1,000 per year. Now, suppose you can borrow an additional $10,000. With your original $10,000, you are now able to buy a $20,000 piece of property. Suppose further that you can still earn 10 percent but are paying 8 percent on the borrowed $10,000, then

Borrowed	$10,000
At 8%	0.08
Cost of borrowing	$ 800
Earning on	$20,000
At 10%	0.10
Gross earnings	$ 2,000

Effect of Leverage

Gross earnings	$2,000
Cost of borrowing the $10,000	800
Net earnings	$1,200

It easily can be seen in the illustration above that, as a result of leverage, you've increased your earnings from $1,000 to $1,200. And all is well.[1]

This is an illustration of a one-to-one leverage ratio. In other words, the equity capital is $10,000 (amount you put up) and the amount borrowed is $10,000. Most investors compute this as the ratio of earnings to equity. You put up $10,000 worth of equity capital on which you netted $1,200; thus

---

[1]Large corporations have been doing the same thing from day one. They float bond issues. (When a corporation sells a bond, it is really borrowing.) With the money borrowed, the corporation hopes to earn a greater return than the cost of borrowing.

Ratio of earnings to equity = $\dfrac{\$1,200}{\$10,000}$ = 12% return on the $10,000 equity

You can lever on more than a one-to-one ratio. The ratio can be one to two, one to three, or whatever. Suppose you are involved in a one-to-two ratio. This means you are going to borrow twice your equity—$10,000 equity capital to $20,000 borrowed capital. Then the leverage would look something like this:

Borrowed	$20,000	
At 8%	0.08	
Cost of borrowing	$ 1,600	
Earning on	$30,000	
At 10%	0.10	
Gross earnings	$ 3,000	

Effect of Leverage

Gross earnings		$3,000
Cost of borrowing the $20,000		1,600
Net earnings		$1,400

Ratio of earnings to equity = $\dfrac{\$1,400}{\$10,000}$ = 14% return on the $10,000 equity

In real estate investments, the above leverage ratio, namely, the one-to-two ratio, is very common.

Can leverage work in reverse?

You bet, and this is something to be wary of. *But unlike many other types of investment, it need not be disastrous* —painful, without a a doubt—but disastrous infrequently.

How does it work in reverse?

In the example given above, the assumption was that you were able to borrow at 8 percent and earn 10 percent on both your equity and the amount borrowed. Suppose you can still borrow at 8 percent, but have miscalculated and earn only 7 percent instead of the hoped-for 10 percent. This means that you earn 7 percent on not only the borrowed amount but your equity capital as well. In a one-to-one–ratio situation, the result would look like this:

Borrowed	$10,000
At 8%	0.08
Cost of borrowing	$ 800
Earning on	$20,000
At 7%	0.07
Gross earnings	$ 1,400

Effect of Leverage

Gross earnings		$1,400
Cost of borrowing the	$10,000	800
Net earnings		$ 600

Ratio of earnings to equity = $\dfrac{\$600}{\$10,000}$ = 6% return on the $10,000 equity

This is still not a disaster. You would have been better off simply investing your original $10,000 equity at 7 percent, earning $700, instead of borrowing the other $10,000.

However, reverse leverage can be fatal if the borrowing is too highly levered. It is possible to have a *negative* return on a highly levered investment. As an example, if the investment is an apartment building and a large number of vacancies occur, the owner not only may not receive a return on his or her $10,000 investment, but when payments on principal plus interest on the borrowed money are included, may also need to pay money out of pocket.

If the investor cannot meet these payments, foreclosure may be the result.

Here's another good thought about leverage.

Good things sometimes do happen in real estate investments—again, mainly as the result of inflation. For example, rents that cost $46 per month in 1945 cost $100 per month for the same unit in 1969, an increase of over 100 percent.[2] Rent rises will probably continue from 1975 onwards until at least 1979, the reason being that the high interest rates that began being required in late 1973 to early 1974 are rapidly resulting in a chronic shortage of single-family residences and multiple dwellings. The increasing demand for housing, the housing shortage, and rising inflation will lead to large rent increases. If operating expenses can be held lower than rent rises, the percentage returns on levered properties should double or even triple in the near future.

What is cash flow?

Cash flow is one of the favorite buzz words of the real estate investor—an important and frequently misunderstood concept. By definition, *cash flow* is the amount left over to the investor after interest, payment on the principal, and all operating expenses have been paid. In short, cash flow is the amount the investor can *spend*. Sellers of investment properties frequently expound the virtues of cash flow to make properties attractive, but cash flows must be analyzed with care. A typical cash flow statement is shown in the example on the following page:

---

[2]*Economic Indicators*, Council of Economic Advisors, 1969.

The Broken Arms Apartment

Income
  Gross income $10,000
  Less: vacancy allowance of 5%   500
Effective gross income $9,500

Operating expenses
  Real property taxes $ 500
  Insurance   200
  Maintenance   100
  Utilities   500
  Management   500
  Miscellaneous expenses $1,000
Total operating expenses $2,800

Other expenses
  Interest payments   3,000
  Payment on principal   1,000

Total expenses   (6,800)
Cash flow $2,700

A word about the separation of the interest payment and payment on principal is necessary before we go further. In the example, the interest is $3,000 and the payment on principal is $1,000, totaling $4,000. Taken together they constitute another real estate investor's buzz word, namely, *debt service*. Debt service is the amount that must be paid back to the lender monthly, annually, or for whatever time period has been agreed upon. In the illustration, the annual debt service is assumed to be $4,000. The logical question then is why split the debt service into its component parts? The reason is that, for tax purposes, interest is regarded as an expense while payment on principal is not. Payment on principal is part of taxable income.

This makes just plain common sense. If payment on principal were regarded as an expense and hence as a deduction, no one owning real estate investment property would ever need to pay taxes. All such persons would have to do would be to set up their debt service so that every dollar after operating expenses would pay off the principal, and they'd be home free. But the IRS doesn't allow this.

Getting back to the illustration, we've concluded that the cash flow is $2,700. Looks pretty good? Maybe, maybe not. That depends a great deal on how much cash you put down on the property and, of course, on your tax situation, as will be dealt with later.

What about the ratio of cash flow to down payment?

For purposes of illustration, let's exaggerate a bit. Suppose you paid $100,000 down on a piece of property and your cash flow was $2,700. The ratio between cash down and cash flow is expressed as a percentage: $\frac{\text{cash flow}}{\text{cash down}} =$ percentage return on cash down. Using the figures given above, then $\frac{\$2,700}{\$100,000} = 2.7\%$. This isn't a very good percentage of cash flow to cash down when the down is $100,000. As a matter of fact it's grim.

Now assume a cash down of only $10,000 and a cash flow of $2,700; then $\frac{\$2,700}{\$10,000} = 27\%$. This, of course, looks much better.

Warning One: It's perfectly possible to have a negative cash flow. This means that you've paid out more than you've taken in; consequently the percentage return on cash down may be expressed as a negative figure. This situation might be, repeat might be, all right depending on your tax situation, as we'll see later. But most certainly it will hurt if it goes on for too long.

Warning Two: *Normally* when borrowing from a financial institution on commercial property, you can expect a loan-to-value ratio of 66 2/3 percent. This means that the lending institution puts up two-thirds of the appraised value of the property, and you put up one-third.

For purposes of illustration, assume there is a $30,000 investment property. Your cash down is $10,000, and the institution lends you $20,000. Your gross income is $5,000 a year. After everything is paid, the amount spendable, or cash flow, is $1,000. Then you figure your cash flow to cash down: $\frac{\$1,000}{\$10,000} = 10\%$.

Here is another illustration. Suppose that for one reason or another, your gross income is reduced 10 percent. If all other costs remain the same, your cash flow will go down by $500, or 50 percent. Why? If all other expenses remain the same and your gross decreases from $5,000 to $4,500, the reduction has to come from your cash flow. Thus $\frac{\$500}{\$10,000} = 5\%$ return on cash down. This is painful but not terribly harmful.

But trouble may come with a cash down that is *too* low. Assume the same situation as described in the first example: a $30,000 property with $10,000 down. Somebody advises you to put only $5,000 of your own cash down and to borrow the other $5,000 on a second mortgage. Suppose the payments on the second mortgage are $500 a year. You still gross $5,000 a year, but your expenses have gone up $500, and as a result, your spendable cash flow is $500. Then $\frac{\$500}{\$5,000} = 10\%$. Still the same as it was before and not really too bad.

Now assume that your gross income is reduced 10 percent, or $500—then what happens? Your cash flow is zero, and $\frac{\$0}{\$5,000} = 0\%$ return on your cash down. At this point, *any* reduction in gross income or increase in operating expenses will move you into a negative cash flow position necessitating out-of-pocket cash payments, possible refinancing, or even foreclosure.

Can cash flows be manipulated by eager sellers?

Indeed, they can and are by various methods. It is absolutely necessary, therefore, to analyze the figures that make up the cash flow.

Rule One: Anything that adversely affects gross income seriously affects cash flow.

In the preceding example, a *10 percent* reduction in gross income reduced the cash flow by *50 percent*. Thus you should make the following study of your cash flow:

1 *Analyze the Gross Rents* Are they really that much, or are they overstated? Look at the books for at least a year.

2 *Analyze the Vacancy Allowance* Is the vacancy allowance truly only 5 percent? It may be at the moment. But what has been the past history of the area? What has been the past history of the property? What are the prospects of growth in the area?

3 *Analyze the Expenses* Are they really correct? True, the real property taxes were, say, $500 this year, but they probably will go up next year. Is there enough insurance coverage, and so on? Will heating costs rise next year? By how much?

Rule Two: Where maintenance has been deferred for a long time, cash flow can be adversely affected. Deferred maintenance is sometimes called *milking* a property. For example, suppose you buy a property and suddenly discover that it needs $5,000 in repairs. True, the previous owner showed a beautiful cash flow, but this may have happened because he or she neglected much needed repairs. Immediately you've got to put up $5,000, thus reducing your cash flow by that amount. Furthermore, you are really paying an additional $5,000 for a property that you might have thought was a bargain.

Rule Three: Carefully examine any and all existing leases. Existing leases may call for abnormally high rents. In addition, they may be ending soon. It may be that you won't be able to rerent the property for the amount previously paid, and consequently your future gross income will be reduced. This reduction in income will lower your cash flow.

Rule Four: Make certain projected rent schedules are for real and are not idle dreams. If you are either building or purchasing a new building, remember that the object of the game is to make a fair return on your investment.

If you are going to have a building built, you will be shown a projected rent schedule by the builder or promoter. You will also see projected expenses and projected net earnings. The projected net earnings may indicate a fair return of, say, 10 percent. But remember, the income to be received on the property can never be estimated to be more than that of like accommodations in a like location. You can't put a luxury apartment house in an area where rents are low. You've got to look to the returns from other similar properties.

In short, it does not necessarily follow that because a certain amount is invested in a property, rentals can necessarily and arbitrarily be established to assure a fair return on the investment. Be realistic in your assumptions, especially if you are making the projections yourself.

Cash flows and tax flows: What's the difference?

At the risk of repetition, cash flow is the amount spendable. Tax flow is the taxable income—or loss—to be carried over to your tax returns. Tax flow and cash flow cannot be the same, except by pure chance. For example, you could put your mortgage payments at an unusually high level and thereby wipe out your cash flow, but this action won't affect tax flow by a single dime. And it's tax flow that is watched by your IRS.

In the final analysis, tax flow can be thought of in this way: Cash flow + payments on principal − depreciation = taxable income (tax flow).

Why include payments on principal? Because every time you reduce the principal, you increase your equity. To be able to exclude these payments from taxable income would be a blatant loophole in the tax laws. If it were possible, you would simply set your mortgage payments (including payment on principal) at a level at which your equity would increase rapidly, and then you would make no tax payments—it just can't be done.

Why subtract depreciation in the above formula? Depreciation is a loss of value and presumably therefore a loss of equity; thus it is a permissible deduction against income.

We've established then that cash flow and tax flow are not the same thing but that cash flow is used to arrive at tax flow. Let's go back to the cash flow statement of the Broken Arms Apartment and use that for an illustration. There we had an effective gross income of $9,500, total operating expenses of $2,800, interest payments of $3,000, and payment on principal of $1,000. Summarized, cash flow and tax flow would look like this:

The Broken Arms Apartment

	Cash Flow	Tax Flow
Effective gross income	$9,500	$9,500
Less: Total expenses	2,800	2,800
Interest	3,000	3,000
Payments on principal	1,000	–0–
Cash flow	$2,700	
Less: Depreciation (assume $2,000)		2,000
Tax flow		$1,700

When you analyze the above summary, the answers to several questions should become clear: (1) Why was payment on principal subtracted from effective gross income in arriving at cash flow? *Answer:* Because it was paid out, leaving that much less spendable, which is what cash flow is. (2) Why was payment on principal not subtracted from effective gross income in arriving at tax flow? *Answer:* Because payment on principal increases equity and thus is considered a part of taxable income. (3) Why was depreciation subtracted in figuring cash flow? *Answer:* It was not subtracted from cash flow because it is not a cash out-of-pocket figure. It is a "paper" figure. It *was* subtracted from effective gross income in determining tax flow because such a deduction is permitted under the Internal Revenue Act. The theory is that the value of the property has decreased through wear and tear—a form of depreciation. Therefore depreciation is a legitimate deduction.

As will be pointed out later in a more complete discussion of taxation, the amount of depreciation permitted depends on the methods used to compute it. In the preceding example, the $2,700 is *spendable*, but because of the excellent tax shelter provided by real estate investments, only $1,700 is taxable. In short, $1,000 is free from taxation.

5 / GUIDELINES AND RULES OF THUMB

There are a number of general guidelines and rules of thumb that can help you analyze any real estate investment. The following discussion demonstrates how they can be used.

All the numerous types of investment properties—each having its own subtleties and complexities—should be analyzed to determine which fills your particular investment needs and expectations. Regardless of the investment property selected, there are two preliminary questions that need immediate answers: (1) What is the zoning? (2) What is the status of the title?

1 Zoning is the restrictions placed on the use of land, generally by a county or municipality. For example, land may be zoned or restricted for use as single-family residential, multiple-dwelling, commercial, and so on. In addition, heights of buildings on particular parcels may be regulated, and zoning regulations may restrict the

amount of land that a building can occupy. In a nutshell, zoning regulations may say that yes, you may build an apartment house on this parcel of land, but it is limited to so many feet in height; furthermore you must construct it so that there are a certain specified number of parking spaces per apartment.

The justification for zoning regulations lies in the police power written into the Constitution of the United States, namely, the government's right, as part of its police power, to regulate the use of land to protect the health, morals, and welfare of the nation's citizens.

Moral: Look before you leap, especially when considering an investment in vacant land.

Copies of local zoning regulations are available in city and county planning offices. By reading the regulations you can readily determine to what use the land may be put. Zoning regulations often can be changed. However, getting them changed is frequently very difficult, and it can be a costly and frustrating experience.

2 The status of title of the proposed investment is extremely important. Are there any "clouds" on the title, such as your seller having a judgment against him? If you buy the property under these circumstances, the judgment passes with the land.

One way to determine whether your prospective title is marketable or merchantable[1] (the term used in the western part of the nation) is to have an abstract of title prepared by an abstract company or an attorney. The *abstract* is the history of the title showing all of the trans-

---

[1]These terms are synonymous and mean that the title is so good that the courts will order its acceptance by a purchaser

actions involving that parcel of property to date. It is examined by your attorney to determine if there are any defects of title. The only problem arises when your attorney makes an error. You're stuck ... unless you can prove that he or she was negligent rather than just making an error in judgment.

Consequently the best thing for you to do is to obtain a title insurance policy. This most certainly will be insisted upon if a financial institution is involved in the transaction. The validity of the title is guaranteed by the insurance company, which is then liable for both its negligence and its errors in judgment, its liability subject only to any exceptions that may be written into the policy.

at should be done before investing?

Before becoming involved in any of the larger types of real estate investments, you must make an economic feasibility study. This rule goes for investing in apartments, office buildings, and shopping centers. The fact of the matter is that with the larger projects, financial institutions won't lend a dime without an economic feasibility study. They need something to make them feel that the project will go before they will part with their money. The institutions may not require the study for smaller projects, but you certainly need it. With the larger projects, the studies are done by professional consultants. As a very, very minimum they cover the following topics:

1 How many people live in an area? What is the population trend? What is the average family size? What are the population ages? People below thirty to forty and over sixty-five years of age are more likely than people in other age groups to rent apartments. Thus the presence of many people younger than thirty living in a

given area might indicate a good demand for rental units.

2 What is the average income of people in the area? People with modest incomes can't afford luxury apartments.

3 What about employment? How many people are employed in the area? What are the sources of employment? What are the employment fluctuations?

4 What sorts of transportation are available?

5 What is the real estate market, in terms of number of projects, dollar volume, and average prices?

6 How many dwelling units are being constructed? What kind of units are being constructed? Are they single-family or multifamily units?

7 How is the land being used within the area? What are the planned uses? What is the average market value by type of use?

8 What sort of zoning regulations, building codes, and land-use restrictions are there?

9 What are the present rents in the area? How do they compare with the expected rents in your proposed project or purchase?

10 What are the vacancy rates? These must be analyzed by type of unit, location, and dollar rental.

11 What are the interest rates? You might want to defer the project until they have gone down.

12 How is the city or town growing? What is the rate of land absorption by type of use? What is the direction of the growth?

13 What is the competition and how is it doing? What are the rents and vacancy rates of your competitors?

The preceding market analysis is by no means complete, but it can be used as a guideline. A professional real estate consultant will go into much more detail.

How do you analyze a particular property?

There's a difference between scheduled gross income and effective gross income. Sellers will show you what amounts to an *annual* income and expense statement. This is scheduled gross income. Often they will suggest that if you buy the property, you will be able to raise rents, say, $5 per month. This suggestion should be taken with a grain of salt. It can be countered with the simple question, "If rents are so easy to raise, why haven't you done it?"

An *annual* income and expense statement can be misleading, particularly with regard to vacancies. Rent rolls minus vacancies equals effective gross income. Okay, on the annual statement prepared for buyers, the seller may have included, say, 5 percent vacancies. But is this figure for real? The only way you can make sure is to ask to see the monthly income and expense statements for the past year from which, presumably, the annual statement was prepared. This is extremely important. Suppose an abbreviated statement is as follows:

Effective gross income	$100,000
Operating expenses	80,000
Net income	$ 20,000

Suppose an *inaccurate* statement was made with regard to vacancies and the number of vacancies was really 5 percent greater; then

Effective gross income	$95,000
Operating expenses	80,000
Net income	$15,000

Note: The 5 percent reduction in effective gross income amounts to a 20 percent change in *net* income. The error in estimating effective gross income is crucial compared with errors that may have been made in the operating-expense statement.

The operating-expense statement also must be carefully analyzed for realism. Suppose, for example, that insurance premiums amounting to $3,000 are included in the operating expenses. Upon analysis, you determine that the property is underinsured. To protect yourself, you'll have to bring the insurance up to the mark. Say the cost of more insurance is $600, or 20 percent of the $3,000. Then your statement will look like this:

Effective gross income	$100,000
Operating expenses	80,600
Net income	$ 19,400

Then as a result of the 20 percent error in calculation of the insurance premium, the change in net income amounts to only around 3 percent. It's not that bad, but it still points up the need for examining all the items making up the operating statement and revising them realistically upward where necessary. After all, *you* are the one parting with the money.

Are there any good rules of thumb?

Yes, there are, and because they are rules of thumb, they are guidelines and guidelines only. They are useful, however, and they apply to various types of properties, so that you can make rapid value judgments prior to a more complete analysis of properties that may be of interest. These guidelines follow:

1 *Interest Rates and Their Movements* Are they going up or down, or are they stable? Generally when interest rates move up, construction slows down, particularly in the area of multifamily-dwelling and commercial construction. This happens because even if builders are fortunate enough to obtain loans they must pay higher rates of interest on the mortgages. Therefore it may be advantageous for you to assume an existing mortgage at a lower rate even if you have to pay a premium for a building.

High interest rates may affect also your decision about the type of property in which you invest. High interest rates generally cause a rise in unemployment. Suppose, for example, that you have been thinking of building an apartment house with units to rent at $150 per month. You've analyzed the market and have found that most of the people living in the area are automobile factory workers and have moderate incomes. At this point, you should ask yourself the following question: "Will rising interest rates lead to unemployment in this particular industry?" If so, perhaps you should forget about that particular property. Higher rates may lead you to decide to build an income-producing property where the rents will be $300 per month, if the property is located in a neighborhood where incomes are high and the possibility of unemployment is remote.

People in younger age groups are usually apartment dwellers, and as a general rule, as disposable income declines for any reason, many of these people double up. However, rising interest rates can be a signal for doubling up on a nationwide basis, *but not necessarily* in the area of your proposed construction.

When interest rates rise, construction activity falls. It follows that a severe housing shortage probably develops within 18 to 24 months. Therefore it might be appropriate to purchase an existing apartment building. Although the building may have high vacancies at the moment, you may decide to purchase it from a disillusioned owner provided the price is right, there is enough income to pay the debt service, and it provides a decent tax shelter.

Rising interest rates tend to stabilize or even lower the price of vacant land. As construction activity declines, the demand for vacant land declines and so, frequently, does the price. If you feel that interest rates will decline in the near future, this may be an opportune time to buy vacant land. One reason is the nature of its financing, which will be detailed later.

If there is a fall in interest rates, mortgage money becomes readily available. Therefore construction activity increases. What's more—lenders frequently lower down payments, thereby increasing the leverage. Generally, too, employment picks up with declining interest rates, and increased employment leads to an increase in the demand for dwelling units. But a period of easy credit may very well lead to overbuilding in certain areas. Consequently a thorough analysis of the market is extremely important.

With the decline in the interest rate comes an increase in the demand for vacant residential land, and the price of this rapidly disappearing commodity shoots up.

2 *The Gross-Income Multiplier* The gross-income multiplier is a rule of thumb designed to express easily the value of a piece of real property. It is a ratio designed to convert rental income into value expressed as a multi-

ple of either annual or monthly gross income. Suppose, you see an ad reading, "Selling price, four times rent." What this means is that the income is capitalized at 25 percent (1 ÷ 4 = 25%).

At this point you might ask what difference the multiplier makes. By itself probably very little. However, if *comparable* properties are selling for five times rent, then the advertised property may be a bargain. Repeat, it *may* be a bargain. Gross multipliers can sometimes be deceiving for the following reasons:

Gross income rather than net income is used. This means that there is no accounting for operating and maintenance costs. One operator may be more efficient than another, thus receiving a greater *net* income working from the same amount of gross income.

There is an implied assumption that all real property taxes, heating costs, etc., are the same.

The remaining economic life of two properties earning the same gross income may be quite different. A gross multiplier approach assumes that the remaining economic life of all comparables is the same.

In any case, the gross-income multiplier is a rough guide to value. It presupposes that you have a knowledge of sales prices as well as gross income of comparable properties.

3 *A Variation of the Gross-Income Multiplier* A variation of the gross-income multiplier is gross income expressed in terms of price per square foot, for an apartment house or an office building, or price per front foot, for a store.

Suppose, for example, that the going market rental for a store is $500 per front foot and there are 50 feet of frontage. Then the gross income is $25,000. If similar properties are going for six times the gross, then the property should be worth $150,000.

Suppose, on one hand, I offer to sell you a property for $150,000 and tell you that it is 50 front feet and is renting for $400 per front foot, or $20,000. If comparables are renting for $500 a foot, then obviously it is overpriced. Six times gross income should price it at six times $20,000, or $120,000, rather than at the $150,000 offering price. At the current rent of $400 it is overpriced, assuming the new buyer can't get the $500 rental.

On the other hand, if I offer you a property with a 50-foot frontage for $150,000 and tell you that the rent is $600 per front foot, this should cause you to brighten up considerably. I'm really telling you that the property is underpriced. In this case the gross income is $30,000, and with a multiplier of 6, the property should be worth $180,000.

4 Margin In real estate investment terms, margin can be best thought of as a cushion. It's a handy tool for analyzing a rental-type investment.

Margin is the difference between 100 percent occupancy and your break-even point. It is the cushion between 100 percent occupancy and the point at which either expenses and the debt service have to be met by out-of-pocket payments or the property is lost. Reduced to a simple formula, it is as follows: Total charges to the investor (debt service + expenses) ÷ gross potential income = margin (allowable vacancy or rental decrease before the need for out-of-pocket payments).

Let's see how it works by looking at the Broken Arms Apartment in a slightly different way.

Gross potential income before vacancy	$10,000
Less: Operating expenses	2,800
Net income	$ 7,200
Less: Debt service (interest + principal)	4,000
Cash flow	$ 3,200

Debt service	$4,000
Expenses	2,800
Total charges	$6,800

Thus $\dfrac{\$6,800}{\$10,000} = 68\%$ break-even point

$100\% - 68\% = 32\%$ margin (allowable vacancy or rental decrease before out-of-pocket funds are needed)

The margin becomes very important when second mortgages are used to finance a sale. Obviously the payments on these seconds must be met, and the payments become an additional part of the debt service. Where this is the case, the margin or cushion can disappear very rapidly with an increase in the vacancy rate.

Assume the same situation as above except that there is a second mortgage on the property and the debt service on it is $2,000 a year. Then

Gross potential income before vacancy	$10,000
Less: Operating expenses	2,800
Net income	$ 7,200
Less: Debt service on first mortgage	4,000
Cash flow after first mortgage	$ 3,200
Less: Debt service on second mortgage	2,000
Cash flow after second mortgage	$ 1,200

Expenses	$ 2,800
Debt service on first mortgage	4,000
Debt service on second mortgage	2,000
Total charges	$ 8,800

$$\frac{\$8,800}{\$10,000} = 88\% \text{ break-even point}$$

100% − 88% = 12% margin (allowable vacancy or rental decrease before out-of-pocket funds are needed)

This figure really means that if the vacancy rate goes over 12 percent, you will have to pay out of pocket.

Any rules of thumb regarding margin?

Obviously, the greater the margin, the greater the safety. Also:

1 A 20 percent margin, or about, is ideal.
2 A 15 percent margin is acceptable.
3 A 10 percent or lower margin is too thin. Beware.

6 / RESIDENTIAL PROPERTIES

Residential-property investment runs the entire gamut from the single-family residence to the multifamily apartment complex. Each type of investment has its own peculiarities in terms of financing, tax advantages, and investment decision making. But in recent years, all types of residential-property investments have been excellent hedges against inflation.

vesting in the single-family residence?

Strictly speaking, the single-family residence, the property to be used as your home, is not considered a real estate investment. But the truth of the matter is that for most people it is the largest single investment they will make. In addition, it has the inherent advantages and disadvantages of other real estate investments; it provides a tax shelter, is protection against inflation, and is relatively nonliquid.

A house on Long Island, for example, purchased for $12,000 in 1953, recently sold for $32,000. The owners not only lived in the house for over 20 years but also used the interest on the loan and the real property taxes as personal income tax deductions. The spectacular price rise took care of inflation. True, the house was relatively nonliquid (it took 90 days to sell), but it also was highly levered. The down payment at the time of purchase was $1,500. Thus it can be said that home ownership is, in a sense, a real estate investment.

What to look for in buying a house.

Many of the same characteristics you look for in any real estate investment. To begin with, look at the trend of the neighborhood. In any city or town, neighborhoods or districts are created, and many of them develop their own characteristics. Most neighborhoods are constantly changing. The changes are mostly from a higher to a lower level of use, bringing about what is known as economic obsolence. Economic obsolence is the impairment of desirability or usefulness of a property brought about by economic or environmental changes in a neighborhood. It often causes a loss in value of a house.

As a rule, look for a neighborhood containing a high percentage of owner-occupied houses as distinguished from rooming houses or rented units. Also, the owner-occupied neighborhoods should contain well-located and well-planned houses built with the same general physical characteristics. An appraiser of real property calls this concept the principle of conformity. Briefly the rule is that the maximum value of real property is found where there is a reasonable degree of homogeneity among all the standards of the area. In short, a lot must be developed much in the same way as the adjacent property. For example, a stucco house in a neighborhood in which other houses were of modern design would stick out like a sore thumb and cause a decline in the value of all the houses. Another example is an extremely expensive one built in a neighborhood of low-cost houses. The value of the expensive house would probably decline shortly after completion.

The second item to look for is *convenience*. This means convenience of the location for the family unit. (The same thing holds true if you're planning the development of an apartment complex.) Here such things as convenience of transportation, schools, shopping areas, churches, and even recreational areas (parks and the like) are included.

w are houses financed?

Houses are financed much in the same way as are other types of real estate investments. Generally some cash down is required along with a mortgage on the balance. By definition, a mortgage is the creation of an interest in real property as security for the payment of a debt or the fulfillment of an obligation.

Typically the borrower (called the *mortgagor*) signs either a promissory note or, in a few states, a bond payable to the lender (the *mortgagee*) in the amount borrowed. A *promissory note* is a written promise by one person to pay money to another. For all practical purposes, a bond is the same thing. Technically a bond is a sealed agreement in writing in which the *obligor* (the borrower) promises to pay under stated terms a sum certain to an *obligee* (a lender).

The other instrument the borrower signs is the mortgage itself or the deed of trust. By virtue of this instrument, the real property is *hypothecated* (a fancy word for *hocked*) as the collateral for the promise to pay.

There are only three basic types of mortgages. However, variations of these have appeared under different labels. The basic types of mortgages are the following:

1 *The FHA-Insured Mortgage* The FHA-insured mortgage is a mortgage that is insured by the Federal Housing Administration, now part of the Department of Housing and Urban Development (HUD). The FHA is an insurance corporation. Rarely does it lend money itself, but it simply insures loans made by approved FHA lenders, which, for all practical purposes, consist of the various financial institutions (the savings and loan associations, etc.). If a person borrows and the deal sours, the FHA pays any loss to the institution upon foreclosure and compliance with FHA procedure.

Standards for accepting applications for loans and for insuring a particular parcel of property are set by the FHA, not by the institutions. There are three basic standards that must be met. First, the property itself must meet certain minimum requirements. These things include lot size, workmanship, etc. Second, the location must be acceptable. Third, persons applying for loans must have earning power and income that will enable them to pay off the loan according to the terms of the mortgage.

The insurance premiums are paid by the borrower and are included in the monthly payments. The rate is ½ of 1 percent of the unpaid balance of the loan. The amount of interest that can be charged by the lender is set by the FHA and varies from time to time.

2 *The VA-Guaranteed Mortgage* The VA-guaranteed loan is commonly referred to as the *GI mortgage*. Veterans of

World War II, the Korean War, and the Vietnam War are eligible as are certain categories of veterans' widows who have not remarried.

On home and farm loans the Veterans Administration may guarantee up to 60 percent of the original mortgage or $17,500, whichever is the lesser. Such loans may be for purchasing, constructing, improving, or repairing the home or farm home owned by the veteran and *occupied by him as his residence.*

Suppose you borrow $20,000 on a GI loan. The institution is guaranteed 60 percent of the loan, or $12,000, in case of default. If the loan is for $30,000 then the maximum amount guaranteed is $17,500.

What the VA guarantee amounts to is a cushion as far as the lenders are concerned, of up to $17,500. Basically, it would be exceedingly difficult for the lender to lose. The down payment can be from zero on up. In the final analysis, the down payment is a matter of negotiation between the lender and the GI.

The interest rates are generally set on a par with those of the FHA loans and also vary from time to time.

On December 31, 1974, President Ford signed the Veterans Housing Act of 1974. The act affects more than 25 million veterans. One important aspect of the new law is that the VA will insure loans in condominium projects. Prior to this it was difficult for a veteran to buy a condominium because under the law, each unit had to have been built under FHA inspection and at least one FHA loan had to have been closed in the project. The 1974 act established the $17,500 maximum amount guaranteed, raising the maximum from the previous high of $12,500.

The act also set the interest rate at a maximum of 8½ percent, but obviously this can be changed.

3 *The Conventional Mortgage* A conventional mortgage is one that is neither government-insured nor government-guaranteed. It is generally different from the FHA and VA mortgages in three ways. First, the interest rates are often higher. The lenders charge what the traffic will bear; and in times of tight money, rates are *high*, with the result that the lower-interest-bearing FHAs and VAs practically dry up. Conventionals constitute the bulk of mortgages both in numbers and dollar volume. Second, the time of payback is generally shorter than with the FHAs and VAs. The institutions like to make mortgages for 20 to 25 years. Third, although the institutions can lend as high as 95 percent of the value of the property on conventionals, they tend to demand higher down payments than on FHAs or VAs. This statement is especially true during periods of tight money.

Recently *privately* owned mortgage-insurance companies have sprung up. Among other things, they insure *conventional* mortgages. In short, if a borrower fails to pay the financial institution from which he borrowed, then the insurance company will bay back the lender. Naturally the borrower pays the monthly premium for the coverage.

One important ruling by the Federal Home Loan Bank Board has been that savings and loan associations can lend up to 95 percent of the value of the property provided that the deal is insured by one of these privately owned companies. As a result of this ruling, there has been a drastic increase in the number of conventional mortgages and at the same time a decrease in the number of VA and FHA loans.

What's a prepayment clause in a mortgage?

Ordinarily a person cannot pay off a conventional mortgage ahead of the due date without the consent of the lender. To obtain the consent the borrower is forced to pay a substantial money penalty. Consequently, borrowers should insist on a prepayment clause in the mortgage which gives them the right to prepay at any time. There will still be a penalty, but it won't be as great as it would be in the absence of this clause.

On May 1, 1972, the FHA suspended loan prepayment penalties. Actually this regulation suspends prepayment penalties to borrowers who pay off their loans before the first 10 years of the amortization period have passed. This action is designed to make the FHAs more competitive with the VAs, which have no prepayment penalties.

Why bother with a prepayment clause?

It could really save you money in the event of a decline in interest rates. For example, suppose you have an existing loan at 9 percent and rates go down to 7 percent. The payoff to you would come if you paid off the existing loan and refinanced the property at 7 percent.

What's a wraparound mortgage?

Strictly speaking, it isn't a mortgage at all. It's a device used mainly as a "sweetener" in the sale of commercial property.

It works like so: Suppose that a prospective buyer of a commercial property has a relatively small down payment, that the seller has an assumable mortgage of $25,000 at 6 percent, and that the property is priced at $75,000. Let's say the buyer has only $10,000 in cash for the down payment. The seller is willing to take back a second purchase-

money mortgage of $40,000 at 8 percent. The sweetener
is that the buyer agrees to assume the old first mortgage
of $25,000 but must be willing to pay the full 8 percent on
it. The seller, of course, is still obligated to pay his lender
only 6 percent.

This means that the effective yield on the $40,000 owed
the seller increases drastically. It means that the seller's
getting 8 percent on $65,000 and thus may be induced to
accept the relatively small down payment in order for the
deal to go through. This mortgage is said to be a *wraparound* because the higher rate is being wrapped around the
old mortgage.

What about variable mortgage interest rates?

Currently there's a movement afoot to place variable interest rates on mortgages. The idea is simple. When borrowers borrow on a mortgage, they must agree to pay the *going
rate*, subject to periodic review. The going rate is to be
tied to a reference rate. One of the reference rates that has
been suggested is the *prime rate*, which is the rate charged
by large city banks to their top credit rated customers. Suppose the prime rate is 10 percent, you borrow, and you
agree initially to pay 2 percent above the prime rate; consequently your mortgage starts out at 12 percent, subject to
periodic review. Suppose then that the prime rate goes up
to 11 percent. You have to pay 13 percent (11 percent +
2 percent over the prime). Conversely if the prime rate declines to 8 percent, you then pay 10 percent (8 percent +
2 percent over the prime).

The fact of the matter is that Federal Land Bank loans on
farms and some insurance company loans on farms are
based currently on a variable rate. In the case of the Federal Land Bank loans, the so-called reference rate is the

rate that it costs the Bank to borrow the money on the open market. A percentage is added onto this.

The variable mortgage rate can be grim for the borrower, and it is a thing to be avoided where possible. For example, suppose you borrow initially at 7 percent and suddenly the rate jumps to 13 percent. Your budget may be unable to hack the difference, and conceivably you could lose your home. Some of the proponents of the variable rates say that you shouldn't worry about that. Why shouldn't the monthly payments be made constant and the time over which the mortgage is due simply be stretched out? This can result in the borrower paying forever and for all practical purposes never paying anything on the principal but just paying the interest on the loan.

ow do seller's discounts work in mortgages?

Seller's discounts are used almost exclusively in FHA and VA mortgages. They are always paid by the seller. It's illegal to charge them to the buyer—directly, at least.

Suppose you sell your house to Jane Smith and, in the contract, she agrees to an FHA mortgage. You go to a financial institution that agrees to give her a loan of $20,000 at a rate of 8 percent. Assume that the market rate is higher than 8 percent (this means that conventional loans are being made at a higher rate). Most certainly the financial institution will tell you it will cost you, the seller, points, for example, 5 points (which really means 5 percent).

What it boils down to is that you will actually receive $19,000 from the financial institution ($20,000 less 5 percent discount). Although you have received only $19,000, your buyer has signed a note and mortgage agreeing to pay back the institution $20,000 at 8 percent. The institution is earning 8 percent on $1,000 that it never paid out.

As a result, its effective yield is greater than 8 percent, the rate carried on the face of the mortgage. In this way, its rate of return tends to equal the market rate, namely, the rate the financial institution would have received had the mortgage been a conventional one instead of an FHA mortgage.

Sometimes sellers try to compensate for the discount either by raising the selling price or, in the case of builders who have to pay the discount, by cutting costs on the house—and maybe reducing the quality of construction.

How else can the residence be financed?

Just like any other investment property. The house can be sold on contract for deed, as was outlined previously. Or, in the case of an existing mortgage, the buyer can assume the seller's mortgage. This also was previously outlined. Or the seller can take back a purchase-money mortgage.

What's a nonassumption clause in a mortgage?

The neatest trick of the week. Invented by, and since about 1969 written into most home mortgages by, the financial institutions. Here's how this clause works. Say you borrow $20,000 on a conventional mortgage at 8 percent. The nonassumption clause says that you can't sell the residence and have your buyer assume the mortgage without the written consent of the institution that loaned you the money. Now you want to sell. You go hat in hand to your friendly financial institution and inform it that you have a buyer who is willing to assume your mortgage. Will the institution give you permission? It depends. It depends on what has happened to interest rates since you bought the property and agreed to pay 8 percent. It boils down to three situations: (1) If interest rates are still 8 percent, the institution will probably say yes. What's to lose? (2) If interest rates have fallen to, say, 7 percent, it will be delighted. Why? If your buyer still wants to pay 8 percent when the market is calling for 7 percent interest, the institution's obviously got it made. (3) If rates have moved up since you bought the property to, say, 9 percent, then obviously the institution won't let your buyer assume at the 8 percent rate. It'll make the buyer refinance at the higher rate, if he or she is qualified.

The big clout available to the financial institutions is the fact that the nonassumption clause is tied to an acceleration clause. Suppose you go ahead and sell the property, permit someone to assume the mortgage, and fail to inform the institution holding the mortgage. The acceleration clause states that in a case like that, the entire balance of the loan becomes immediately due and payable. If it is not paid, the institution simply forecloses on the mortgage.

All in all, it's a neat way for the institutions to have their cake and eat it too. However, employment of this sort of vicious tactic on the part of the institutions has raised considerable indignation among some consumer-minded legislators, who are threatening to introduce bills to prevent it.

To oppose this move, the institutions are threatening to stop making mortgage loans. This is, of course, nonsense, because if they fail to make mortgage loans, particularly if they are savings and loan associations, they will be out of business.

Should down payments on houses be high or low?

Now we're back to leverage again. On houses it's debatable. The arguments go like so:

A large down payment is better, because it reduces the interest payments. Some people argue against this, saying that the saving in interest is not large enough when weighed against the yield possibilities of alternative investment opportunities. Some people argue in addition that the down payment is tied up because the house is relatively nonliquid, at least until the owner is able to sell it for what he or she paid for it.

A small down payment is better, some say, because the interest payments are deductible from the individual income tax, thus partially offseting the interest paid on the mortgage.

Where there is a possibility that the homeowner will have to move, it is better to buy a house with a small down payment, because it is easier to sell a house with a small rather than a large down payment to a person assuming the mortgage.

What's the deal in investing in one-tenant residential realty?

There are a number of forms of one-tenant residential investments. The investment strategy, problems, and possible rewards are surprisingly similar among these forms of realty except for one, which should be gotten out of the way immediately; this form is the condominium. A *condominium* is a form of ownership of real property characterized by the fee ownership of individual units, commonly apartments, coupled with an undivided interest in common in the remainder of the property. Generally condominiums are bought in the same way houses are purchased. The buyer gives a down payment and finances the balance by means of a mortgage. The buyer pays principal, interest, taxes, and insurance on the unit plus an annual or monthly sum for management and maintenance.

Basically there are two types of condominiums, one designed for the individual to own, and if it is an apartment, for him to live in. The purchase of this type is similar to the purchase of a single-family residence.

The other type of condominium is the recreational condominium purchased for recreation and investment. The recreational condominium purchased for investment is undoubtedly the worst type of investment ever invented by mankind. Why? The possibility of leverage of any kind is literally nonexistent. Institutions for the most part require 30 to 40 percent down, and the interest rates are typically higher than on any other type of conventional mortgage loan. You will be informed by an overzealous salesperson about the doctor who owns three units and is making money out of them, although she has never seen them. This is pure nonsense. Physicians are relatively unlearned in financial affairs, but they are not stupid. When given this pitch, run, do not walk to the nearest exit. What the salesperson is really saying is that we in management can rent it for the season. And every recreational area has a season—whether it's ski season, about 120 days, or the winter season in Miami. The property will probably rent for only about *half* the season. If you want to use it yourself during the season or any part thereof, then probably it will be infrequently rented. In short, expect a *negative* cash flow. This means that you'll have to pay out-of-pocket costs. You will be advised that it is a beautiful tax shelter. It *is* a tax shelter. But not much, and man does not live by tax shelters alone.

For the most part the managers of recreational condominiums are a band of ripoff artists whose direct ancestors were horsethieves born on the wrong side of the sheets. They will conveniently fail to credit you with monies during times the unit was rented and will charge you for nonexistent or dubious services. For example, there exists a record of one recreational management firm charging an absentee owner $3.75 for a "mouse call," whatever that means.

You have one possibility, and one possibility only, that the purchase of a recreational condominium for investment only will be a good investment, and even that possibility is doubtful in this day and age of gasoline shortages and rising gas prices. It is the *hope* of capital appreciation. But if there is some capital appreciation, you probably will have difficulty selling the property to someone who will assume the mortgage. The down payment will be exceedingly large, and consequently you will be competing with newer condominiums. Therefore it probably would be best for you to offer the property for sale with a relatively small down payment, take back a second purchase-money mortgage, and hope for the best. Even under these circumstances, the recreational condominium is difficult to sell. The culprit is the gasoline shortage. Builders of new condominiums are finding them more and more difficult to sell, thus forcing prices down on the older properties. *But* if you want a recreational condominium just to play around with—have fun.

Warning: Many, many people were badly burned in the condominium market during the money crunch in 1974 and early 1975. Here's how it happened: A person visited a condominium site under construction. He or she gave the builder a down payment on a partially constructed unit, and the builder promised that the entire project would be completed by a certain date. The builder used the "buyer's" down payment for part of the construction costs and then discovered that, due to tight money, he was unable to obtain further financing. The project remained unfinished, and the builder filed for bankruptcy, leaving the buyers holding the bag for their down payments.

Moral: Under *no* circumstances permit a builder of an unfinished condominium project to hold your down payment. If you want to buy, insist that the down payment be held in escrow (by a banker or other third party). Insist further that the money *not* be delivered to the builder until the project is completed or until the title is closed on your purchase.

w does the single-family house rate as an investment?

It's a good place to start. The main reason is that if the transaction is handled properly, you can get in with very little down, thereby being able to take advantage of leverage. But don't count on this type of investment being too profitable. You *can* expect a fair rate of return, a tax shelter, and a good chance for capital appreciation when you get out.

at are some of the guidelines for investing in a single-family se?

1 Take your time and don't rush in. If you see a house at what you think is an attractive price, shop around the neighborhood, compare sales prices of similar houses in similar neighborhoods. This is one approach to determine the value of a house used by professional real estate appraisers.

How do the appraisers arrive at comparative sales prices? By consulting real estate brokers, multiple-listing bureaus, or title companies, which, for as little as $1.50 a copy, will make copies of the deeds involving sales of comparative homes. Most states have taxes based on the selling price of the transaction, and you can easily compute sales prices of the comparables from the deed taxes. For example, if the tax in your state is $1 per $1,000 of the sales price, then a deed tax of $30 would mean that the house sold for $30,000. The amount of the tax is on the front of the deed.

2 Think about the house in which you may invest in much the same manner as you would think about one you might select as your own home. Consider location, trend of the neighborhood, and other matters previously discussed. Just thinking that someone else is going to have to rent it and live in it is out.

3 Find out what the rents are for similar houses in similar neighborhoods. This information will give you an idea of what you will probably be able to get for the one you have in mind. Also find out if it is customary for the tenants or the landlord to pay utilities.

4 Try, if possible, to buy a house on which the mortgage can be assumed. The reason for this is that with new financing, you are almost certain to become involved with unwanted closing costs and higher interest rates than those on a house four or five years old with an assumable mortgage.

The best mortgages to assume are FHA-insured mortgages or VA-insured mortgages. There are two reasons for this. First, the interest you'll have to pay on both the FHA and VA mortgages is apt to be lower than the interest on a conventional mortgage. Second, the down payment will be lower on a four- or five-year-old home with an FHA or VA mortgage on it than with a conventional mortgage. The reason is that, typically, both FHA- and VA-insured homes are bought with low down payments to begin with, and the sellers don't have time to pay off much on the principal in the first four or five years.

5 Determine the monthly payments. This sounds like a stupid statement. But the real point is to find out if the mortgage is a so-called budget mortgage or not. In many cases, monthly payments are expressed as PITI. This means that part of your monthly lump-sum payment goes for payment of principal, part for interest, part for taxes, and part for insurance. If it's not PITI, then you have to figure that you're going to have to include taxes and insurance as operating expenses.

6 If the down payment is relatively high, ask yourself if you can pick it up by having the seller take back a second purchase-money mortgage. If so, can you get enough rent to make the payments? Using a second mortgage may be advisable if you think there will be rapid capital appreciation in the neighborhood.

7 Are you prepared to manage the property yourself? You should be. Most professional property managers cannot afford to handle single-tenant units unless there are a large number of them. If a professional manager does handle the unit, the costs are generally so high that they use up most of the cash flow generated by the single-tenant unit.

8 Do not get personally involved with your tenants. Personal involvment makes it difficult both to collect rents and to raise rents when necessary.

9 Do as much of the maintenance as possible yourself.

10 Don't forget liability insurance, whatever you do. You've got to protect yourself from a lawsuit. Remember that liability insurance is an expense that you don't ordinarily have in your own home, and it must be treated as an expense.

11 If you own an apartment complex with 100 units and have one vacancy, you have a 1 percent vacancy rate.

If you have a single house and it becomes vacant, your vacancy rate is 100 percent. You've got to be in a position where you can make the necessary out-of-pocket payments over a period of time.

A Big Warning: Under no circumstances should you invest in a single-family house in a neighborhood in which a large percentage of the neighbors work for the same company or factory. A layoff, even a temporary one, spells disaster for property values. Often people who are laid off will place their homes on the market. What's worse—those people still working may feel that they are the next to lose their jobs and may also place their homes on the market. Home values tend to collapse, but fast, in this situation.

What's the situation in the duplex to sixplex range?

Again, select the property in much the same way as you would go about selecting your own home or the single-family residence to be used for investment. In short, the emphasis is on location, neighborhood, and trend of the neighborhood. Pay particular attention to the availability of public transportation. Even before the day of the gasoline crunch, public transportation was important, particularly to senior citizen tenants. (They need public transportation to get around and frequently will rent in an area because good transportation is available, and remember that older tenants tend to stay put longer than younger people.) If you intend to live in one of the units, keep in mind that the tenants will be your neighbors. Remember, too, that if you do occupy one you can save on management costs.

As a cardinal rule, select your unit as if you were going to sell it for a gain a few years down the road. If you do sell, be careful not to overprice it. Again, shop similar properties in similar neighborhoods to find out the comparative sale prices.

hat sort of financing can be had on these units?

Generally, the financing is good and relatively easy to obtain, especially if one of the units is owner-occupied. The institutions look mostly at your ability to pay come what may. If your credit is good, they will lend the money with a relatively small down payment, which, of course, gives you greater leverage.

On the older duplex to sixplex investments, much of the financing is done with the seller taking back a second purchase-money mortgage and the buyer assuming the existing mortgage held by the financial institution. This arrangement may amount to an exceedingly small down payment and a high leverage ratio. *But* make certain that you have the ability to meet the payments if the cash flow should become negative.

In these deals, the second purchase-money mortgages are set up in one of three ways, each with a different degree of risk. Payments of principal and interest on the second mortgage may be set up over a relatively short time period. This means that monthly payments are apt to be high. Payments on principal and interest may be set low for a relatively short time period (usually five or seven years) and then after you've paid off part of the principal for, say, five years, you make a balloon payment of the balance. With this arrangement you should be certain you'll either have the money to pay or have the ability to refinance the property at that time. You may be required to pay the interest only for five or seven years, and then you'll have to come up with the entire balance due. With this arrangement also, you have to be certain that you'll either have the money or can refinance at that time. Remember, interest payments are generally higher on second mortgages than on first mortgages. The reason is that the lender's risk is greater.

Warning: Recently, retired or semiretired older citizens have been sold fourplexes with sometimes pretty sad results. The sales pitch has been that the fourplex is small enough to manage yourself. You can live in one apartment and rent out the other three. You'll have enough to make your monthly payments and have some tax-free cash flow to supplement your retirement income. This is fine when the owner-occupant has some cash reserves to cover contingencies. But retired or not, don't count on 100 percent occupancy. Don't be sold on a pro forma income statement showing a 100 percent occupancy rate. In the real world, 100 percent occupancy over time is the exception rather than the rule.

Remember, one vacant unit in a fourplex means a 33 1/3 percent vacancy rate, not counting your apartment. Be on the safe side in calculating income and expenses. Figure on the possibility of the one-third vacancy rate, and hope that over the year there will be only about a 10 percent vacancy rate. Then ask yourself if you have the necessary funds to carry the project.

How about investing in apartment buildings?

The term *apartment house* can cover a broad spectrum of multifamily units ranging anywhere from eight to eight hundred or more units. In the smaller units, the owner is frequently the manager and/or resident manager. The larger units are typically managed by professional managers who in turn supervise the resident manager.

In nearly all cases, the project begins with a builder-developer who builds and then immediately resells to an investor. In many cases the builder sells to an investor prior to construction. Generally apartment houses are financed with a construction loan coupled with a long-term mortgage commencing upon completion of the building. The larger units are often financed through the creation of a limited partnership, organized through the efforts of a promoter of limited partnerships. Sometimes they are financed through money borrowed from real estate investment trusts.

hat are the opportunities in residential rehabilitation?

Rehabilitation consists of remodeling older buildings with the objective of increasing their yields. Generally the opportunities are excellent. What's more, rehabilitation is a chance for a person of modest means to get into real estate investment. Once the property is remodeled, the investor can either rent it or sell it for a profit.

Rehabilitation financing is provided for under Title II, Section 220 of the national housing act. The loans are insured and consequently are risk-free as far as the lending institutions are concerned.

Consult a financial institution about the possibility of obtaining such a loan *before* you commit yourself to the purchase of the older property. Remember, the institution doesn't have to make a loan even if it is insured. What's more—the institution will not loan you any money unless it feels that your loan will give it a favorable return.

Some states grant aid to rehabilitation, the idea being to

increase the supply of decent rental housing. New York State, for example, has a statute authorizing cities to adopt ordinances that provide that any increase in assessed valuation resulting from alterations (eliminating unhealthy or dangerous conditions) in *certain multiple* dwellings will be exempt from local property taxes for a period of up to 12 years. Check your local state statutes and/or city ordinances to see if this sort of thing exists in your area.

In addition, the 1969 tax act allows a special fast write-off on rehabilitated property. Again the reason being to increase the supply of rental housing (much more about the tax aspects later).

7 / COMMERCIAL AND INDUSTRIAL PROPERTIES

Commercial and industrial properties are not given the more favored tax treatment of residential properties. Nevertheless they do provide excellent cash flows, some tax shelter, and, often, opportunities for capital appreciation.

What about a store as a one-tenant commercial realty investment?

Stores are a risky business. For the most part, they're difficult to finance, they're hard to keep rented, and, what's worse, downtown business districts of cities and towns have a bad habit of jumping—a good business district one year may be a bad district the following year.

If you're lucky enough to have a tenant with a national credit rating who has a long-term lease, fine. (A tenant with a national credit rating would be a company like

Sears or General Motors.) Otherwise you are a pure land speculator, hoping to cover your costs while waiting for someone to buy the building in order to put the land to another use. Without a long-term lease from a reliable tenant, your best chance for success is to try to buy cheap and hope for a decent cash flow.

How are commercial leases arranged?

Most commercial leases are one of three types or a combination of the three.

1 *The Gross Lease* Here the tenant pays a flat sum, generally monthly. Out of this the landlord pays all the expenses of the property and keeps whatever's left over. This is like the typical apartment lease (although in many cases the apartment tenant pays either all or part of the cost of utilities).

2 *The Net Lease* Here the tenant pays all the expenses including taxes and gives the landlord a flat sum each month. This is the typical arrangement made when a piece of vacant land is leased to a franchise. The landlord receives a net. If taxes, water charges, and so forth go up, the tenant and not the landlord pays the increases.

3 *The Percentage Lease* Many business leases are done on this basis. The landlord receives a percentage of the tenant's gross income. If the tenant's business income increases, the landlord's income rises. If the tenant's income decreases, the landlord's income declines.

The percentage lease is often coupled with what is in the nature of a gross lease. For example, say you receive 10 percent of the gross; if this doesn't amount to a sum greater than, say, $300 per month, then you are guaranteed the minimum of $300.

The percentage paid is generally determined through negotiation between the landlord and the tenant. But there are two general rules that are followed: The higher the markup on the merchandise sold in the store, the greater the percentage paid. For example, the owner of a jewelry store where high markups is the rule pays a high percentage. The faster the turnover of the merchandise, the lower the percentage paid. For example, the owner of a grocery store where markups are low and turnover is fast pays a low percentage.

How good is a shopping center as an investment?

Like investing in the subdivision and the high-rise office building, investing in a shopping center takes know-how and a large amount of capital.

What kinds of shopping centers are there?

To begin with, a shopping center is defined as any area in which a large number of stores of various types are located and in which a majority of consumers' wants may be satisfied.

Shopping centers are broken down into five general types:

1 The Regional Shopping Center This has a major department store occupying at least 100,000 square feet. Total store area within the center ranges between 250,000 and 1,000,000 square feet and is located on a 50- to 100-acre tract. The regional center is located off one or more traffic arteries and needs a trade-area population of upwards of 200,000 persons to support it.

2 *The Community Center* Here there is a junior department store occupying 25,000 to 90,000 square feet, total store area is between 100,000 and 400,000 square feet on 15 to 20 acres, and the center is supported by a trade-area population of about 100,000.

3 *The Large Neighborhood Center* Here a variety or clothing store occupies 10,000 to 20,000 square feet, total store area is between 50,000 and 100,000 square feet on a 10- to 20-acre space, and a trade-area population of between 20,000 and 30,000 is necessary.

4 *The Small Neighborhood Center* This has a supermarket with 20,000 to 30,000 square feet, generally includes a drugstore or a hardware store, is located on 5 to 10 acres, and requires a trade-area population of between 5,000 and 10,000.

5 *The Superregional Shopping Center* Here there are two to four major department stores with an aggregate area of 1/2 million or more square feet, specialty apparel stores of up to 200,000 square feet, and other stores containing 300,000 square feet. The center stands on 100 or more acres and frequently has space for office buildings and apartment buildings. It needs at least 100,000 persons and an estimated annual income of 1 billion dollars for its support.

How are shopping centers financed?

Mostly through insurance companies or REITs and sometimes even through pension funds.

But: Financing is rarely obtained prior to a commitment from at least one prime tenant with a top credit rating agreeing to a long-term lease. This requirement puts shopping-center developers over a barrel. In short, no lease, no financing, no shopping center. Of course the major tenants are fully aware that the developers need them. Consequently they are in a position to negotiate an extremely low percentage lease together with other favorable concessions. As a result, most of the money made by the developer (investor) has to come from the smaller tenants in the center who don't have top credit ratings.

Furthermore, many lenders require a relatively short time period for amortizing the loan—often requiring what proves to be a dangerous balloon payment at the end. Refinancing, necessary when the balloon is due, may prove disastrous. In addition, in periods of tight money, lenders may force the investor into a participation.

The fact that shopping-center developers are many times at the mercy of Triple A credit-rated tenants often increases the final cost of construction. Construction can't begin unless a permanent mortgage commitment is obtained, and the mortgage takes more than the normal time to negotiate because the developer must get the lease first. In the meantime he or she is probably paying interest on previously financed vacant land.

at are some shopping-center investment rules of thumb?

1 Check the zoning. This goes without saying regarding the site you are considering. But *also* check nearby sites. Why? Because shopping centers often breed their own competition. If business booms in one shopping center, then others may cluster around it, becoming parasites living off the traffic generated from your center.

2 Do a market survey. Have it done by a professional. At the very least it *must* report a breakdown of area population by age, by income, by buying habits. It should include also an analysis of the competition, the accessibil-

ity of the proposed site, and the economic stability of the population. (Is there a good employment mix? If all the people in the trade area work for a single employer and that employer shuts down, you're in trouble.)

3 Your projected income and expense statement must show a return of at least 12 to 18 percent on your cash down; otherwise forget it.

4 The mortgage has to run for at least 10 years; hope for and negotiate for a longer term.

How do office buildings stack up as investments?

The high-rise office building is for the specialist, for the high-risk taker, and not for the faint-hearted. The financing is difficult and costly. (For the most part, the lenders are life insurance companies.) Much like in the financing of shopping centers, the lenders demand that at least part of the office building be leased to Triple A tenants before they will agree to part with a dime. Again, the tenants know this, with the result that they strike a hard bargain with the developer.

One of the problems is that you have to lock the tenants into at least a 10-year lease, hoping to get your investment back by that time. Today's new building is considered an old building by the time it is 10 years old, and Triple A tenants tend to move to new buildings. The main reason for their moves is that they like the prestige of a new building. If they move, they may leave you stuck. However, many of the smaller tenants may be ready for expansion, provided you've properly maintained the building.

It should be mentioned that in the larger cities, many of the office buildings are corporate owned and occupied. More often than not, prestige is the important factor in the corporation's decision to own its own buildings.

It is almost impossible for the builder of an office building to estimate his or her costs with any degree of accu-
racy. The cost of erecting the basic structure or shell is
easy to estimate, but final cost estimates are almost impossible. The reason for this is that the tenants (again the Triple As) demand that their interior design requirements be
met. If they want a bar in the executive suite, you build
them a bar—and it had better be a posh one.

Furthermore, the lapse between the time you start construction and the date of completion will be at least a cou-
ple of years. It can be disastrous if you don't fill the building with other than the original Triple A tenants in the
meantime. In addition, any slowdown in the economy during this time period can leave you with a high vacancy
rate and possible bankruptcy.

Many people lacking the expertise and finances to invest
in the high-rise office building think in terms of the
smaller specialty building. This is the so-called professional building in which doctors, dentists, and lawyers
are likely to be the tenants. Here the problems are not
much greater than the problems involved in financing
and building a six- or twelveplex. However, some of the
financial institutions may require a larger down payment
for a specialty building than for an apartment building.
The reason is that the institutions consider many of these
buildings "single-purpose buildings," and they are extremely wary about the possibility of a relatively high vacancy rate.

You may think of a potential investment in, say, an office
building containing 12 units to be sold as condominium
offices to business executives. To do this properly, you
most certainly should arrange for financing for the sale
(permanent financing) of the individual units prior to construction. A good selling point is that owning a condomin-

ium office gives the owner-occupant the special tax advantage of being able to deduct taxes, interest, and depreciation. Further, a condominium office is an important hedge against inflation, and the building probably will appreciate over time, in case the owner-occupant wants to resell. This sort of investment can be particularly attractive to accountants, attorneys, and insurance people, especially if the building is located in a growing suburban area.

8 / VACANT LAND AND FARMS

Many of the really big gains and losses in real estate have resulted from vacant-land speculation. Because of the negative cash flow in holding vacant land for appreciation, location and timing are extremely important.

Some land speculators prefer holding farmland rather than vacant land because farmland generates cash flow and a greater tax shelter than vacant land provides. But both have unique investment problems.

What about the political climate in the area under consideration?

In many parts of the nation today, land use and land development are severely restricted. Much of the restriction has come about where people are concerned with ecology and such things as "zero population growth."

Much of the restriction on growth has been through zoning and city planning. Most communities have adopted so-called master plans. And anyone thinking of speculating in vacant land must certainly be familiar with the master plan for the community. Briefly, the purpose of the plan is to guide and accomplish a coordinated, adjusted, and harmonious development of the municipality and its environs. The plan tries to make adequate provisions for traffic, light, and air and a more convenient distribution of the population.

The goals of the master plan are accomplished basically by zoning. Zoning means the division of a municipality or county into districts for the purpose of regulating the location and use of buildings, land, and building construction.

It follows then that anyone thinking of getting into vacant land should be familiar with the master plan as well as the zoning regulations.

There are two major types of land investors: land speculators and subdividers and developers.

The Land Speculator: A *land speculator* is hoping to make money from a change in the use of the land. The key to success or failure lies in the way in which the land is financed. The speculator tries, where possible, to use the option (discussed in Chapter 3). The speculator risks the cost of the option and gambles on a 1-year to 18-month change in the land use, figuring that the changes will come about because of rapid population growth and high employment opportunities.

Unless you are an astute market analyst, you should seek professional consultation, because without it you are apt to be burned in land speculation. Just because a new factory is coming into the area doesn't mean you're necessarily going to make good. For example, a developer offered a land speculator in Florida a handsome profit on a parcel of land. The speculator and the developer both had heard that a new factory was coming to town. The speculator held out for a higher price. Then the roof fell in. It turned out that the plant was going to be almost 100 percent automated, hence there would be very little in the way of employment. The developer pulled back, and the speculator was stuck. Had the speculator found out what *sort* of factory was contemplated, the property would have been sold to the developer. It was a case of the blind leading the blind.

The objectives of the land speculator are to get in and get out with as much profit as possible, as quickly as possible, and to get as much leverage as possible; in short, to use the other person's money. The reason the speculator has to get in and out as soon as possible is that time constantly works against the land speculator. Time costs money in terms of taxes and interest. Anything that has to be held more than five years is almost certain to be a loser, especially if cash has been paid for the property. Unless, of course, there has been some sort of fantastic rise in property values.

For example, suppose you have $1,000 to invest. You have alternatives of, say, investing in land or lending the $1,000 at compound interest. Assume that you could lend it out at 7 percent interest compounded. Seven percent is a modest amount in this day and age. At the end of five years, the interest compounded on the $1,000 would amount to over $402.50. If you had paid $1,000 cash for a piece of real estate and had held it for five years, you would be required to pay taxes of, say, $15 per year, or $75. In order to break even, you'd have to get $1,477.50—$1,472.50 covers the $1,000 cash selling price, $75 tax cost, plus loss of $402.50 in interest. This would put you right back to the 7 percent return, which is no big deal for the amount of risk and the nonliquidity to which you've exposed yourself.

Suppose the same situation, but that you were able to sell at the end of one year. Then you could break even at $1,085, the $1,000 being your capital, the $70 being the interest you could have had (economists call this an *opportunity cost*), and the $15 being the amount you paid in real property taxes.

Suppose that in each of the two land-purchase situations above, the price of the property doubled to $2,000 and you got out

1 At the end of five years:

Selling price	$2,000.00
Cost	1,477.50
Profit	$ 522.50

You'd have a gain of 52.25 percent.

2 At the end of one year:

Selling price	$2,000.00
Cost	1,085.00
Profit	$ 915.00

You'd have a gain of 91.50 percent.

3 It can be argued that example 2 is to a large degree unrealistic because of the 100 percent gain in the land value in one year versus 100 percent gain in five years. Assume that the land gained 20 percent per year in value, then at the end of the first year:

Selling price	$1,200
Cost	1,085
Profit	$ 115

You'd have a gain of 11.50 percent, which probably isn't enough in the light of the risks involved. Consequently you should analyze the property in terms of the net percentage gain over and above opportunity costs and real property taxes which you feel is necessary to attract you to the investment over a one-year period, a two-year period, and so on.

How is leverage used in vacant-land sales?

Speculators rarely pay 100 percent cash. More often than not, they try to lever the property as highly as possible. In general, this is done (other than by the option) in one of two ways.

The buyer puts down a small percentage of the purchase price, and the seller takes back a purchase-money mortgage. In one situation, the seller agrees that the buyer need pay *only* the interest for a specified number of years and after that start paying on the principal in addition to the interest.

In the other situation, the buyer puts down a percentage of the purchase price, the seller takes back a purchase-money mortgage, and right away the buyer starts paying interest and principal monthly, semiannually, or annually.

For example:

1 The seller agrees to sell you a parcel of property at $1,000 with 10 percent down, 10 percent interest, and

no payment on principal for five years. Suppose that at the end of five years the price doubles and you get out; then your opportunity cost is still $402.50 (the loss of compound interest), your taxes are $15 per year, and the total cost is $477.50.

Selling price		$2,000.00
Less: Opportunity cost	$402.50	
Taxes	75.00	
Interest	450.00	
Land cost	1,000.00	1,927.50
Profit		$ 72.50

This is a net gain of 7.25 percent.

2 Suppose again that the price of the property doubles within a year; then

Selling price		$2,000
Less: Opportunity cost	70	
Taxes	15	
Interest	90	
Land cost	$1,000	1,175
Profit		$ 825

This is a net gain of 82.50 percent on the $1,000 investment.

In the last analysis, much of what an individual can do depends upon the bargaining positions of the parties involved. For example, if the seller is not too eager to sell, he or she may demand a much higher down payment and thereby may reduce the amount of leverage available to the buyer. Furthermore, the seller may demand a higher rate of interest. If things get out of hand, of course, no bargain can be struck.

Warning: Be certain, if you do invest in vacant land, that you will be able to cover interest, taxes, and additional payments where necessary. Also keep in mind that while the interest and taxes you pay during the holding period are deductible, any gain must be reported on your income tax after you have sold the land for a profit.

The Subdivider and the Developer: A *subdivider* is one who buys undeveloped land, divides it into smaller parcels, and sells it. A *developer* is a person who carries the process a step further and adds homes or other on-site improvements, such as condominiums or shopping centers. Subdividing and developing is a highly specialized area of real estate investment involving much red tape—government regulations often involving such diverse matters as environmental impact statements and zoning regulations—and a dangerous trip up a financial river. It is best left to the experienced full-time operator, not the average investor.

Are farms and ranches good investments?

Recently they have been excellent investments from the viewpoints of both capital appreciation and tax shelters (subject to the post-1969 *hobby farming* tax rules discussed later). In some parts of the country, prices of farm properties have gone up sharply between 1973 and 1975 —frequently up 50 to 100 percent. For example, an Iowa soybean farm bought in 1972 for $212,000 with a $61,000 down payment sold in late 1974 for $400,000, and during the holding period it spit out a 38 percent cash flow.

One of the biggest advantages of owning the farm and holding it for capital appreciation is that it does generate income, often high enough to make the annual payments, and it sometimes generates cash flow.

Most farms held for capital appreciation are farmed on shares. The typical arrangement is that the person doing the farming receives two-thirds of the crop and the landowner one-third. Typically, too, the actual farmer pays for the seed and the fertilizer. An alternative arrangement is for the owner to hire a farmer who is paid a salary and is furnished with the farm home free of charge. In this case, of course, the owner must be ready to furnish the equipment, which in this day and age is extremely expensive.

Warning: Income on a farm is normally generated only once a year: when the crop is sold. But you must also be able to meet any necessary monthly expenses, such as fuel bills, hardware, and other maintenance items throughout the entire year.

9/ DEALING IN REAL ESTATE SECURITIES

In a pure sense, real estate securities are not real estate. However, they involve real estate and often provide profitable investment opportunities. They cover such things as sale-leaseback mortgages, tax certificates, and buying at mortgage foreclosure sales.

w does the sale-leaseback rate as an investment?

It can be great provided that the lessee is the right tenant.

But first . . . a *sale-leaseback* involves the sale of a parcel of real property that is then leased back to the original owner. The buyer then becomes the lessor and the seller the lessee.

For example, suppose a chain store company builds a building costing $100,000. The company then sells the building to an investor for $100,000 and leases it back. Thus the seller-lessee's original capital of $100,000 is freed. Normally the seller-lessee goes ahead and builds another store, thus increasing the size of the chain.

In a real-life situation the property would probably have a mortgage against it bearing a fairly low rate of interest. The reason is that the seller (the chain) would probably have a good credit rating. This mortgage would be assumed by the buyer-landlord, the favorable rate of interest on the mortgage assumed being one of the inducements in the decision to purchase the property.

This sort of transaction has advantages and disadvantages to both parties. The buyer-lessor can depreciate the property, thereby taking advantage of the tax shelter, and also deduct any interest payments plus the real property taxes. Typically these lease arrangements are long-term and are set up so that the rent received by the buyer is greater than the cost of the property over the term of the lease. This means that if the lease is renewed at the end of the term, the rate of return received by the buyer-lessor is fantastically high. Even if the lease isn't renewed, the property is still that of the buyer-landlord, who can sell it and take a long-term capital gain.

As far as the seller-lessee is concerned, capital is freed as indicated above; also the rent paid is a deduction as an ordinary expense. Often the seller-lessee is able to sell the property at a profit over construction costs and take advantage of the long-term capital gains tax. Furthermore, during the time of holding the property prior to the sale, the seller-lessee is able to take interest on the mortgage and real property taxes as deductions.

Warning: Don't forget that as the buyer-lessor, you're tied to both the credit rating and the management ability of the seller-lessee. If the seller-lessee goes belly up, you may be in trouble.

Special Note: If the seller-lessee goes bankrupt, the Chandler Act limits your claim to one year's rent in case of general bankruptcy but three years' rent in case of reorganization. This gives you time to look around for another tenant. After all, the property is still yours.

How do you deal in mortgages and contracts for deeds?

This can be done in various ways. Some investors simply lend money on first or second mortgages at the going rate. For example, if you lend $20,000 on a first mortgage, you simply have the borrower sign the note and mortgage, and the borrower gives you monthly payments of principal and interest. But if you are willing to lend money on a *second mortgage*, you are entitled to a higher rate of interest because your risk is greater. Moreover, you should be in a position to protect yourself in the event of a foreclosure. Basically there are two situations.

(1) Suppose a property is valued at $100,000 with an existing first mortgage of $50,000 on which you take back a $20,000 second mortgage. Remember, you have to be certain that if you have to foreclose, you will be able to pay the $50,000 to the existing first mortgagee. You can't just wipe him or her out.

(2) Suppose the same situation, but the first mortgagee starts to foreclose. If the property brings only $50,000 at the sale, you'll be wiped out. Therefore, again, you've got to be ready to pay off the holder of the first mortgage.

Can this sort of investment be dealt in indirectly?

Yes. On any Sunday, the classified advertisements in any city newspaper advertise both first and second mortgages for sale as well as first and second contracts for deeds. Typically the mortgage or contract is advertised at a discount.

Often the ad reads, "well-seasoned mortgage." The term *well-seasoned* means that the mortgage has been on the property for some time and a good part of it has been paid off. For example, assume that a property is valued at $15,000 and the original face value of the mortgage was $10,000; if all that remains due and payable is $5,000, then it is certainly well-seasoned. The property owner's equity is $10,000 ($15,000 − $5,000 due = $10,000). Thus if you should have to foreclose, the cushion of the property owner's $10,000 equity ordinarily would be enough protection to you, the purchaser of the mortgage.

What is a discount?

It is the balance due on the mortgage less some percentage figure. Say $10,000 is due, and a mortgage is offered to you at a 20 percent discount (sometimes called a *20-point* discount). This means that you pay the mortgage holder $8,000. The borrower, of course, has to pay off the $10,000 due plus whatever interest rate was called for in the original paper. The discount drastically increases your yield.

Warning One: This type of investment offers no protection against inflation and does not provide a tax shelter.

Warning Two: Anyone engaging in this type of investment has to know the fundamentals of residential appraising or else must hire an appraiser. The mortgage may amount to more than the market value of the property, or, put another way, the cushion may not be as great as you are led to believe.

Warning Three: How do you know how much is really due on the mortgage? Suppose the owner of the mortgage lies to you?

This sort of problem arises in the following way. Suppose I offer to sell a mortgage which I own myself. I tell you that the borrower owes me $20,000 on the mortgage but I'm willing to discount it to you for $15,000. How do you know that there really is $20,000 due?

Most mortgages have or should have an *estoppel* clause written into them. Simply, the estoppel clause states that the borrower will, at the request of the lender, furnish a written statement "duly acknowledged" of the amount due on the mortgage as of that date and whether any off-sets or defenses exist against the mortgage debt.

In some states this statement is called a *certificate of no defense*. Once the borrower states the amount due and further states that he has no defense in the event of foreclo-sure, he is said to be *estopped*. The borrower *cannot* later assert in court that he does have a defense or that the amount due is different from what is stated on the estop-pel certificate.

an money be made by investing in tax certificates?

Yes ... if—and a big *if*—you know what you're doing. Here's how it works. If a person fails to pay his real prop-erty taxes, then his property is put up for sale. Each county annually conducts tax sales. A brief description of the property, along with the amount due and the date that the county treasurer will conduct the sale, is advertised.

The first thing to recognize is that the purchaser at the sale does not—repeat *does not*—receive the property even if he or she is the successful bidder. The high bidder re-ceives a *tax certificate*. The taxpayer has from three to five more years, depending on local state law, within which to redeem the property. Suppose that you are the success-ful bidder at the sale, paying delinquent taxes of $1,000.

To hold the certificate you must stand ready to pay $1,000 in year two, another $1,000 in year three, and another $1,000 in year four. That means that you'll have $4,000 invested in the certificate. At this time you will bring what amounts to a foreclosure proceeding, and you'll get the property. *But* don't count on it. Less than 1/10 of 1 percent of the purchasers of tax certificates ever get title to the property.

Then why bother? Because the taxpayer has to pay you the tax you paid plus interest in the event that he or she redeems the property prior to the date of the tax foreclosure proceeding. The money made by investors in tax certificates is made by getting *interest* in most cases, not by obtaining title to the property.

Typically the interest rate paid is high, and typically it is on a sliding scale. For example, in some states it's 18 percent annually for the first six months, 12 percent annually for the second six months, and 9 percent annually thereafter.

Suppose you pay $1,000 for the certificate, and the taxpayer redeems in exactly six months. Then he or she has to pay you $1,090. If the property is redeemed at the end of one year, then he or she pays you $1,150. (Your $1,000 + $90 interest for the first six months + $60 interest for the second six months = $1,150.)

The bidding at the tax sale works just like any other auction. Suppose there's a certificate up for sale and taxes due are $100. You bid $100, I can come up with a bid of $101, somebody else bids $105. Assume that the third bidder gets the certificate. Even though this person paid $105 for it, the taxpayer, upon redeeming the tax certificate, has to pay the certificate owner *only* the $100 due on back taxes plus interest on the $100, *not* interest on the $105.

This means that if you get carried away, the return on your investment declines very rapidly.

Assume, for example, that the high bidder does pay $105, that the rate is 18 percent annually for the first six months, and further that the taxpayer pays off the taxes in exactly six months. How much does the purchaser get? He gets $100 due in back taxes plus six months interest at 18 percent annually, or $109. All well and good. *But* the high bidder paid $105 for the certificate, or, put another way, a $5 premium was paid. This means that the high bidder netted $4 on a $100 investment for six months. Thus for all practical purposes, the yield was cut from 18 percent to 8 percent ($100 × 8% = $8 per annum, or $4 for six months).

Moral: If you get carried away in the bidding and bid too high a premium, you can cut your yield down to nothing or even to a loss. For example, assume the above, except that the taxpayer redeems in three months instead of in six months. In this case the taxpayer has to give the certificate owner only $104.50 for something for which $105 was paid. This is no way to invest. The object of the game is profit.

One important feature in buying tax certificates is the fact that there is little or no risk. After all, the security is the property, and the real property taxes are only a fraction of the market value of the property.

Most states figure the property tax on a percentage of the market value, or "cash" value, of the property, as many of the state tax statutes put it. For example, suppose a house is worth $30,000; some state laws provide that the tax shall be figured on 30 percent of the value, or $9,000. The levy is against the $9,000. This means, of course, that if you do wind up with the property after the statutory time has passed, you will have paid only a fraction of the market value for it.

How do you deal in mortgage foreclosures?

Mortgage foreclosures, if handled properly, can be very profitable. In all states where a mortgage or deed of trust is being foreclosed, the lender has to advertise the foreclosure prior to the sale. Generally the sales take place at the courthouse of the county in which the property is located. The advertisements are run in either a local newspaper of general circulation, a local "legal" newspaper, or both.

The ad gives, among other things, the name of the lender, the name of the borrower, and the date and amount of the *original* loan (not the amount due). The number and page of the book in which the mortgage is recorded are also advertised.

The first thing to do is to copy the original mortgage from the record book or, better still, obtain a copy of the instrument from a title company. The fee for this is very nominal and is well worth it. Then calculate the amount due on the loan. Sometimes the exact amount due can be had from the lender or the public trustee in those states using the deed of trust.

The next step is to look at the house or other property being foreclosed on. The chances of actually getting inside the house are pretty slim, because the person being foreclosed against is probably upset (to put it mildly) about the whole affair. Try to estimate the market value of the property. The quickest way to do that is to find out sales prices of similar homes in similar neighborhoods. Often you can obtain these figures from local real estate brokers or a multiple-listing bureau run by a local Board of Realtors. Sometimes, too, financial institutions such as savings and loan associations keep records of comparative home sales prices.

Remember that you're going to have to pay cash at the time of the sale. Often several small investors chip in, so that the small investors have a chance to get a piece of the action. Another source of funds is often the commercial bank, which may or may not take a six-month note, depending on your credit rating. The bank loan will give you a chance to buy the property and an opportunity to refinance by means of a mortgage.

At the sale, the lender bids the amount due him or her on the mortgage. For example, suppose $15,000 is due. The lender bids the $15,000, plus reasonable attorney's fees, plus advertising and other expenses of the sale. Say this amounts to a total of $16,500. To get the property you'll have to top this. Remember that the borrower (the person being foreclosed) gets the surplus over the amount due on the mortgage. If you bid $17,000, this means the borrower gets $500.

Warning: Mentally you've got to set a top price . . . a bid over which you *will not* go. Don't get carried away. Many, many people do at an auction. After all, you're trying to come out with a profit. As an investor, you're probably not there to buy a new home.

What happens after the sale?

If you're the high bidder, you'll get either a referee's deed or a deed from the public trustee (a trustee's deed) depending on the state in which the sale is held.

But: The delinquent borrower still has a period of redemption. This means that he or she has from 75 days, in some states, to a year, in others, in which to redeem the property or buy it back from you. You'll get your money back. If you bid a sum greater than the sum owed, the lender receives only the amount owed. Any surplus is the borrower's; consequently the borrower has to give you the amount of your bid so that everybody comes out even.

In some states you can't get possession of the property until after the time for redemption has elapsed.

To avoid this delay, most people dealing in mortgage foreclosures approach the borrower and ask for a quitclaim deed. In short, they point out that the entire amount due must be paid in cash by the end of the redemption period. They then offer the borrower $200 or $300 for a quitclaim deed. In the quitclaim deed, the foreclosed borrower says in effect, "I give you what I've got."

For all practical purposes, if the borrower signs the deed he or she waives the right of redemption and also agrees to give you immediate possession. This gives you a chance to fix up the property, if necessary, and to offer it for resale immediately.

Warning: Unless the property is rented rather than sold by the successful bidder, the opportunity for a tax shelter is strictly limited and any profit from the sale will probably be taxed as ordinary income.

10 / TAXATION AND TAX SHELTERS

Tax savings and real estate investments seem to go together like ham and eggs. The tax saving in real estate investments gives this type of investment its double-barreled appeal—tax saving plus an inflation hedge. This statement is true for residential real estate as well as for income-producing real property.

ow does the tax saving apply to residential property?

For the average homeowner there are two main ways. (1) The real property taxes you pay are deductible on your individual income tax return. (2) Any interest paid on a mortgage, deed of trust, or contract for deed is also deductible. In this day of high interest rates, this deduction markedly reduces the effective rate of interest.

re profits from sales of residences taxable?

It depends on what's done with the money. There's no immediate tax (it's deferred) if you buy a new residence within one year at the same or a higher price or if you build a new house with the money within 18 months of the prior sale.

For example, say you bought a house in 1965 for $20,000, sold it today for $25,000, and then bought a new house for $29,000. The $5,000 profit ($25,000 − $20,000 = $5,000) is not taxable because you bought a new house at a higher price. *But,* your Uncle Sam the Tax Man gets you in the end. For tax purposes, the cost, or the base, of the new house is figured at $24,000 ($29,000 − $5,000 profit = $24,000). This means that when you finally sell the new house, for, say, $40,000, you pay a tax on $16,000 ($40,000−$24,000 adjusted base =$16,000 taxable profit). If the taxpayer builds a new home within 24 months of the prior sale, the tax on the profits from the sale of the prior home can be deferred.

How else can the base be adjusted?

The *base* or *basis* is the starting point for determining a gain or loss on the sale of property and for computing depreciation. Normally this basis is cost with some adjustments, but if property is acquired by gift, inheritance, or in some other manner, then a basis other than cost is used.

In a residential sale the base can be adjusted in three ways. You can adjust for the cost of improvements, for fixing-up expenses, and for selling expenses.

What are costs of improvements?

These are considered as being things in the nature of capital improvements or what are sometimes referred to as improvements of a "substantial" nature. Improvements such as a new furnace or fireplace as distinguished from a pane of glass in a window.

at are fixing-up expenses?

Expenses for work done to aid in the sale of the property. Redecorating would be an example. But to qualify, the work must be done during a 90-day period immediately prior to the sale and must be paid for on or before 30 days after the sale.

at are selling expenses?

Such things as legal fees, brokerage commissions, or payment for a title policy or abstract of title.

Suppose you paid $20,000 for a home in 1965 and you sell it today for $25,000, then

Cost of old home		$20,000
Cost of improvements (assume $1,000 furnace)		1,000
Fixing-up expense (assume $500 paint job)		500
Selling expense (assume $1,500 commission)		1,500
Adjusted base		$23,000
Selling price	$25,000	
Less: Adjusted base	23,000	
Net profit or so-called recognized gain	$ 2,000	

Note: If a taxpayer is sixty-five or older before the date of the sale and if the taxpayer used the property as his or her personal residence for a period, whether continuous or interrupted, totaling at least five years within an eight-year period ending on the date of the sale, then the taxpayer is given special consideration.

The special consideration is an exclusion of $20,000 of gain if the adjusted sales price or adjusted base is $20,000 or less. If the adjusted sales price is greater than $20,000, then the exclusion is the proportion of $20,000 over the adjusted sales price.

Suppose a taxpayer over sixty-five sells his or her personal residence with an adjusted sales price of $30,000; then the taxpayer may exclude the proportion of $20,000 over $30,000, or 2/3, of the gain.

How many times can the tax on the sale of a personal residence be deferred?

Any number of times *provided* that you do not make more than one transaction per year and that your new residence is *not* purchased and resold before you sell your older house.

How is the tax figured on the profit?

The amount of tax depends on whether or not the transaction is considered a long-term or a short-term capital gain.

What is a long-term capital gain?

By definition a *long-term capital gain* is the gain on an asset held in excess of one year. A *short-term capital gain* is the gain on an asset held for one year or less.

What difference does it make?

Short-term capital gains are taxable as ordinary income. For example, assume that a person in a 40 percent tax bracket makes a $1,000 profit on a short-term transaction. But if the taxpayer has a long-term capital gain of $1,000, an important change was made in the Revenue Act of 1978. After October 31, 1978 the change took effect.

There is now a deduction of 60% of the gain with the remaining 40% of the gain being taxed as ordinary income.

Assume you have a long-term gain of $1,000 and that you are in the 40% tax bracket, then:

1 $0.60 \times \$1,000 = \$600$ on which no taxes are paid.
2 The remaining $400 taxable as ordinary income, then $\$400 \times 0.40 = \$160$, the amount that you pay in taxes.

Sale of a Personal Residence The 1978 Act provides some good news for some people when selling a personal residence. If you sell your home after July 26, 1978 and are 55 years of age, you may exclude from gross income the first $100,000 of gain.

This exclusion *only* applies if you owned and occupied the residence as your principal residence three of five years preceding the sale.

Can gains and losses be offset?

Where short-term gains and losses are involved, the problem is fairly simple. They may be offset.

For example, you buy a property and sell it three months later for a gain of $5,000. You then sell another short-term property for a $3,000 loss. Your net short-term gain, taxable as ordinary income, is $2,000 ($5,000 − $3,000 = $2,000 gain). If you had come out with a net loss, you could deduct it from your ordinary income. You may deduct a maximum of $1,000 of short-term loss each year.

But there are limitations on the way that long-term losses may be written off. As a general rule, it takes $2 of long-term loss to offset $1 of ordinary income. Up to $1,000 of the loss may be deducted each year. (The unused portion may be carried over as a loss the following year.)

Example 1 Assume

Short-term loss of	$4,000
Long-term gain of	$2,000

Here you have a net loss of $2,000. Only $1,000 may be written off in one year. The other $1,000 may be carried over to the next year.

Example 2 Assume

Short-term loss of	$500
Long-term loss of	$900

Here you can deduct the net short-term loss of $500 plus

one-half of the $900 long-term loss, or $450, for a total of $950, from ordinary income. Nothing is carried over to the following year.

Example 3 Assume

Long-term loss of	$4,500
Short-term gain of	$2,500

Here you have a net long-term loss of $2,000. Your deduction from ordinary income is $1,000. No carryover. The reason is that it takes $2 of long-term loss to produce $1 of deduction from ordinary income, thus using up the full $2,000 loss.

Often ads offering real estate for sale read, "29 percent down." What does this mean?

Actually the ads are referring to an *installment* sale. An installment sale is a method of deferring payment of the tax on the sales price. The fact of the matter is that a transaction may be reported as a deferred payment if two requirements are met. (1) There is no payment in the year of the sale (other than the down payment). (2) Payments in the year of the sale do not exceed 30 percent of the selling price, and payments are made in two or more installments.

Then why do the ads read, "29 percent down"? Probably because sellers want to make certain that they come under the 30 percent rule.

How does an installment sale work?

Suppose you sell a property for $100,000 with an adjusted base of $50,000. This means that your profit is $50,000 ($100,000 − $50,000 = $50,000). Your reason for making the installment sale in the first place is to defer paying tax on the entire $50,000 in the year of the sale.

Assume that you do sell the place for $100,000, with $20,000 down and four annual payments of $20,000 (for illustrative purposes ignoring any interest on the balance). Then

Year 1	$ 20,000 down	your gain is	$10,000
Year 2	20,000 paid	your gain is	10,000
Year 3	20,000 paid	your gain is	10,000
Year 4	20,000 paid	your gain is	10,000
Year 5	20,000 paid	your gain is	10,000
	$100,000		$50,000

Total price is $100,000, of which your total gain is $50,000.

Suppose the same situation as above and that you've held the property for one year or more at the time of sale. Then the tax paid on each year's gain of $10,000 is figured as a long-term capital gain. If the property has been held for less than one year at the time of sale, the profit is considered as ordinary income and is taxed as such.

*ow do you convert residential property to income-producing *operty?*

The reason for doing this is to enable yourself to take advantage of the special tax advantages applicable to "income" property.

Sometimes the conversion of a residence into income-producing property is quite clear, but sometimes there is a gray area that may be questioned by the IRS. Obviously if you rent out your residence for, say, a year, then clearly in that year at least, it will be classified as income-producing property. But if you rent it out for less than the fair market rent for the area, then the IRS will probably challenge your deductions. In short, the IRS will look at the "intent" of the taxpayer. Charging less than a fair market rent is a manifestation of intent.

If a person properly rents out his residence for part of the year, then a proportionate amount of the year's depreciation is allowed. Assume that you own a house and that it is rented out permanently—clearly, then, it has been converted to a rental unit, and clearly you are entitled to a depreciation allowance. The question that arises is on what price is the depreciation figured. The answer is the fair market price at the time of the conversion or the original cost of the residence, whichever is less. For example, if the house cost $30,000 10 years ago and is now worth $40,000, you have to depreciate it from the $30,000 base.

For residential property converted to income-producing property after July 24, 1969, and having a useful life of 20 or more years, the deduction of accelerated depreciation is limited to the 125 percent declining balance method. (Accelerated depreciation or the so-called fast write-off will be detailed later.)

What is depreciation?

In the strict sense of the word, it is a loss of value from any cause. Generally it is referred to as a percentage figure. For example, you might say that a building is 20 percent depreciated. Put another way you are really saying that the building is 80 percent good.

On real property, the loss of value comes from three causes or a combination of these causes. They are physical depreciation, functional obsolescence, and economic obsolescence. Physical depreciation arises from natural wear and tear—a roof sags, metal erodes, or paint cracks, for example. Functional obsolescence is an impairment in desirability and usefulness brought about by changes in design, art, process, and the like. The owner has little or no control over loss of value from this cause.

Economic obsolescence is a loss of value arising from economic forces. Again the owner has little or no control over the loss of value. For example, suppose that you've built a house in a nice, quiet neighborhood. Suddenly the flight pattern from a nearby airport is changed so that the airplanes constantly fly directly over your house. The probabilities are great that your house will lose value.

ow is depreciation handled for tax purposes?

Accountants recognize that wear and tear does take place, and they do provide an entry for this sort of return of capital. The dollar amount of depreciation, however, is not actually "paid" to anyone. On a building, for example, it is a paper deduction, allowable every year. It is allowable only on the building because the concept is that land does not wear out and thus doesn't depreciate.

More important—the IRS recognizes that depreciation occurs. Thus if you have an income of, say, $15,000 per year, from an apartment house and you are permitted a *write-off* of $10,000 as depreciation, you pay tax on only $5,000 ($15,000 − $10,000 = $5,000). In a sense, the $10,000 is tax-free. Furthermore, if you have income amounting to $25,000 aside from your income from the apartment house, then you are taxed on $25,000 + $15,000 = $40,000 − $10,000 depreciation, or on $30,000.

The IRS has established guidelines for depreciation as shown in the table below.

Useful Life in Years[1]

Types of Buildings	Useful Life in Years
Apartment Buildings	40
Banks	50
Dwellings	45
Factories	45
Garages	45
Grain Elevators	60
Hotels	40
Loft Buildings	50
Machine Shops	45
Office Buildings	45
Stores	50
Theaters	40
Warehouses	60

Remember that the above table refers to *useful life* new. An older building may have a useful life, or *remaining economic life* as it is often called, of only 10 years. In this case the depreciation is based on the remaining economic life of the building.

How is depreciation figured?

For all practical purposes, the IRS recognizes three methods of figuring depreciation. They are the straight-line method, the declining-balance method (of which there are several variations), and the sum-of-the-digits method.

How is straight line figured?

This is the simplest form of write-off permitted the taxpayer. An equal amount each year, after salvage value is taken into account, may be deducted. For example, assume a building valued at $20,000 with a salvage value

---

[1]Internal Revenue Service, "Revenue Procedure 62-21."

estimated at $8,000 and a remaining economic life of six years. Then $20,000 − $8,000 salvage value = $12,000. Then

$$\frac{\text{Unrecovered costs}}{\text{Useful life}} = \text{Rate of depreciation per year}$$

In this case

$$\frac{\$12,000}{6 \text{ years}} = \$2,000 \text{ per year}$$

If this building were later sold by you for $15,000, then the basis on which the new owner will compute taxes is $15,000, regardless of how much you had previously depreciated the structure. The new owner's basis definitely would *not* be your cost minus your depreciation, but his or her cost. *Note:* If you own the property for only part of the taxable year, you can depreciate it for only the time you hold it. For example, if you own it for nine months, your depreciation is three-quarters of the whole year.

The declining-balance method

There are three variations of this *fast write-off* method used in depreciating real estate, but the basic principles are the same.

The 200 percent declining-balance method permits the taxpayer to depreciate at double the straight-line rate during the first year. For example, suppose a building (not including the land) is valued at $100,000 and has a remaining economic or useful life of 10 years. In the straight-line method, you would depreciate 10 percent per year, or $10,000 annually. However, in the 200 percent declining-balance method, you can double that amount, to $20,000 the first year. This leaves $80,000 to be depreciated the second year, or 20% × $80,000 = $16,000 deducted the second year, leaving a balance of $64,000. Then 20% ×

$64,000 = $12,800 deduction the third year, and so on. But: The property *cannot* be depreciated below the salvage value. Assume that the salvage or scrap value is estimated at $5,000. When you've depreciated it down to that figure, you can go no further.

The other fast write-off variations of the declining-balance method of depreciation are the 150 percent declining-balance and 125 percent declining-balance methods. Regulations require the use of these two methods under certain well-defined conditions, as will be pointed out later.

In the 150 percent declining-balance method, the write-off is simply one and a half times the straight-line rate. For example, assume again that the building is valued at $100,000 with a remaining economic life of 10 years. The straight-line depreciation is 10 percent per year. Using the 150 percent declining balance, the rate is 15 percent per year. Thus $15,000 is written off the first year, leaving $85,000. The second year $12,750 is written off, and so on. If the 125 percent method is used, depreciation is simply at the rate of 12½ percent per year.

The sum-of-the digits method

The rate here is determined by a fraction according to the Internal Revenue Code "the numerator (of which) changes each year to a number which corresponds to the remaining useful life of the asset (including the year for which the allowance is being computed), and the denominator which remains constant is the sum of the years' digits corresponding to the useful life of the asset."

Thank goodness, this official gobbledygook can be reduced to a formula:

$$\frac{\text{Remaining economic life}}{\text{Sum of the years of useful life at acquisition}}$$

For example, assume the $100,000 building with a remaining useful life of 10 years and a scrap value of $10,000. The denominator is the sum of the years, or

$$1 + 2 + 3 + 4 + \ldots + 10 = 55$$

Then

$$\frac{10 \text{ (remaining useful life)}}{55 \text{ (sum of years of useful life at acquisition)}} = \frac{2}{11}$$

The value of the building used to figure depreciation in this method is $100,000 − $10,000 (scrap value) = $90,000.

Thus

First year's depreciation $= \frac{2}{11} \times \$90,000 = \$16,363$ rounded off

Second year's depreciation $= \frac{9}{55} \times \$90,000 = \$14,724$ rounded off

This procedure is continued for the balance of the 10-year period.

How is real property classified for tax purposes?

In one of four ways: (1) for sale to customers, (2) for use in a trade or business, (3) for the production of income, (4) as property held for investment.

1 *For Sale to Customers* Where property is held for sale to customers, the individual taxpayer is treated like any other merchant. For example, a real estate broker may buy and sell on his own account. If the broker does so, all he may deduct are interest payments, real property taxes, and expenses involved in the sale. If the broker does receive income from the property, he may deduct depreciation subject to the rules of *recapture* (like anyone else), as will be explained later.

2 *For Use in a Trade or Business* This type of property covers a store, factory, farm, office building, or the like. Here the taxpayer may naturally deduct her real property taxes as well as her interest payments. The taxpayer may deduct depreciation also, as well as ordinary expenses. If the taxpayer sells the property at a gain or a loss, the sale is subject to the short- or long-term capital gains regulations previously discussed.

3 *For the Production of Income* Here real property must be shown to be held for the purpose of producing current income. Taxes, interest, expenses, and depreciation of improvements may be deducted. Any losses may be carried over to be offset against income from other sources.

4 *Property Held for Investment Purposes* A parcel of real property is bought with the intention of selling it at a gain. All gains or losses are treated as either long-term or short-term capital gains or losses. Interest, taxes, maintenance, and repairs are deductible. No depreciation allowance is permitted because presumably the depreciated property isn't producing income. In most cases the property being held is vacant land.

How did the 1969 act affect the rules of depreciation?

The 1969 act made some drastic changes regarding depreciation of real property. To begin with, real property was divided into nonresidential real property and residential real property. Different depreciation rules apply in each instance.

1 *Nonresidential Real Property* This is commercial property, industrial property, and such recreational property as bowling alleys. On this type of property constructed or put under a binding contract after July 24, 1969, the

maximum fast write-off is the 150 percent declining balance. But this fast write-off applies to only the *first* owner. All subsequent owners must use the straight-line method.

2 *Residential Property* The 1969 act defines residential property as any building of which at least 80 percent of the gross income is received from the rental of dwelling units, excluding transient units such as hotels and motels.

The act also regulated depreciation of new construction and used construction, applying special rules to each category. With *new construction* the *first* owner may choose the method of depreciation. The 200 percent declining-balance, 150 percent declining-balance, sum-of-the-digits, or straight-line method may be used. However, in the event of sale, the *excess* depreciation, meaning that amount over and above straight-line depreciation, is taxable as ordinary income if the property is sold at any time prior to 100 months of ownership.

For example, suppose you took the 200 percent declining balance, during the first year wrote off $8,000 for depreciation, and then sold the property. The straight-line depreciation would be $4,000. The extra or *excess* $4,000 ($8,000 − $4,000 = $4,000) would be taxable as ordinary income.

The regulations affecting *used construction* mean that second and subsequent owners of residential construction have special rules regarding fast write-off depreciation. If the property has a remaining useful life of 20 or more years, owners may use the 125 percent declining-balance method of depreciation. If the property has a remaining useful life of less than 20 years, then the owners *must* use the straight-line method of depreciation.

A word about recapture.

Recapture is the excess depreciation recouped. This is taxable upon the sale of the property.

The 1976 Internal Revenue Act taxes the recapture depending on time of holding of the property as well as the type of property (residential property as contrasted with government assisted projects).

The "recapture" is the excess over straight line depreciation. For example, suppose a double-declining balance figures out to $3,000 depreciation while, under straight line, it would have been $1,000, then $2,000 is "recaptured" and taxed ($3,000 − 1,000 = $2,000).

The 1976 Internal Revenue Act taxes the recaptured money depending on the time of holding the property as well as the type of property (residential property contrasted with government assisted projects).

There are basically three situations under the 1976 Act

1   *Property held between 12/31/63 through 12/31/69.*

Depreciation Claimed	"Excess" Depreciation Recapture Percentage	Minimum Time of Holding to Avoid Recapture
	100% of "excess" depreciation—1% for each month over 20 months.	No recapture if held 120 months

For example, assume property is bought July 1, 1964 and sold July 1, 1967. Assume you depreciated it at $3,000 but the straight line would have been $2,000. What is your "excess" on which you will be taxed? *Answer:* $3,000 − $2,000 = $1,000. You held the property for 36 months.

Thirty-six − 20 months = 16 months × 0.01 = 16%; then $1,000 × 0.16 = $160. The taxable excess is then $1,000 − $164, or $836.

The $836 is taxable as ordinary income in addition to whatever tax is applicable to your profit.

2 *Property held between 12/31/69–12/31/74.*

Depreciation Claimed	"Excess" Depreciation Recapture Percentage	Minimum Time of Holding to Avoid Recapture
1. All real property except 2 and 3 below.	100%	None. No matter how long you hold it.
2. Gov't assisted projects constructed and acquired after 1975.	100% of "excess" depreciation–1% for each month held over 20 months (this is the same as 1 above)	120 months
3. Residential rental property to 12/31/74	100% of "excess" depreciation–1% for each month over 20 months (this is the same as 1 and 2 above)	200 months

3 *Property held after 12/31/74.*

All excess depreciation over straight line is taxable as ordinary income, no matter how you depreciate.

The question comes up as to how recapture is handled if, say, you buy the property in 1968 and sell it in 1980. This is extremely complicated and a good tax accountant or tax lawyer should be consulted.

What are the special rules regarding rehabilitation?

To encourage rehabilitation of older residential dwellings, Congress provided some special tax incentives under the 1976 Act.

You can write off the cost of rehabilitation in five years by using the straight-line method, and you can disregard salvage value. The rehabilitation cost per unit must be greater than $3,000 to qualify, but it must *not* exceed $20,000 per unit. Remember that you can write it off in five years even though the estimated useful life is greater than five years.

For example, you spend, say, $20,000 for rehabilitating a unit having a 10-year life. You can use five years. Thus

$$\frac{\$20,000}{5 \text{ years}} = \$4,000 \text{ per year allowable depreciation}$$

What happens if the rehabilitated unit is sold?

It all depends on the timing. (1) If you sell the property within 12 months or less, *all* of the write-off is labeled "excess" depreciation and is taxed as ordinary income. (2) If you sell the property after 12 months but in less than 100 months, all excess write-off over the true straight line is said to be recaptured and is taxed as ordinary income.

This means that whereas you were permitted to depreciate a rehabilitated property in five years, the rules of the game change when a sale takes place.

Suppose your cost is $20,000. You are permitted to give the property an arbitrary useful life of five years. *But* on the sale, the real remaining useful life must be figured.

Suppose it turns out to be 20 years; then the real straight-line-depreciation period is 20 years and the depreciation has to be computed at $1,000 per year instead of the $4,000 per year. Now suppose that you sell at the end of two years. Under the five-year rule, you would have taken $8,000 in depreciation ($4,000 per year for two years). However, the real straight-line depreciation is $2,000. In this case, then, the excess depreciation is $6,000, and this amount becomes taxable as ordinary income.

Like in any other fast write-off, if the property is sold after 100 months the amount subject to recapture decreases at the rate of 1 percent per month.

What are tax-free exchanges?

Strictly speaking, there is no such thing as a tax-free exchange. What this type of deal amounts to is a situation in which the tax is deferred or postponed. The Internal Revenue Code states, in effect, that real or personal property that is used in the trade or business of or held for investment purposes of the taxpayer qualifies for this sort of postponement if it's exchanged for "like kind" of property.

What is "like kind" of property?

Trading an apartment house for an apartment house is ordinarily held to be an exchange of "like kind" of property. Decisions in some tax cases have been that the exchange of a farm for city property qualifies as does that of a commercial property for unimproved city lots and even that of domestic real property for foreign real estate.

Why bother with an exchange?

Suppose you brought a piece of real estate for $50,000. You've depreciated it down to $30,000. Assume that it has appreciated to $100,000 in value. If you sell it, at the very least it will be subject to a long-term capital gains tax of $70,000 ($100,000 − $30,000 = $70,000). This figure doesn't include the possibility of excess depreciation.

If you traded it even for another property worth $100,000, you would still have a gain; however, the gain would not be taxable at the time of the exchange. You would defer paying the tax. In addition, you could depreciate the newly acquired property.

But if you resold the newly acquired property for, say, $110,000, the basis for determining your tax would be the depreciated value of the old property minus any depreciation you might have taken on the newly acquired property. Say the depreciation on the newly acquired property amounted to $10,000. Then the $30,000 basis (or value after you depreciated) of the old property minus $10,000 depreciation on the new property = $20,000, the adjusted basis of the property. The net result where the selling price was $110,000 would be $110,000 − $20,000 = $90,000. That would be the amount on which the tax would be computed.

Suppose mortgages are exchanged in a trade?

This situation comes about like so. You own an apartment building currently valued at $100,000, but it cost you $75,000. You trade with Mr. Smith for an apartment house valued at $250,000 which has an assumable mortgage of $150,000. The basis of the newly acquired building then becomes $225,000:

Basis of old apartment house	$ 75,000
Mortgage assumed by you	150,000
Basis of newly acquired building	$225,000

At this point there is no taxable gain as far as you are concerned. The general rule is that the amount of the mortgage debt assumed is treated as cash.

But suppose you sell the building for $300,000 within a year; then

Selling price	$300,000
Basis of the apartment house	225,000
Taxable gain	$ 75,000

Mr. Smith is faced with a somewhat different situation. Assume that the adjusted basis of the apartment house that he traded with you was $175,000 (valued at the time of the trade with you at $250,000). Then

Value of the apartment house received from you	$100,000
Mortgage assumed by you	175,000
	$275,000
Less: Value of the apartment you received	225,000
Taxable gain to Mr. Smith is *now*	$ 50,000

What happens if boot is given?

Obviously in real life, things are not wrapped in neat little packages. Most trades are *not* on an even-up basis. Typically one of the parties involved has to throw in a little *boot* money in order for the trade to take place.

Boot can consist of cash or "unlike" property. Now if you transfer a piece of real property with an adjusted basis less than the value of the property you receive, the difference is a gain. This gain is recognized to the extent of the cash received plus the fair market value of the unlike property.

For example, you exchange a large apartment building for a smaller one plus cash of $20,000 and $80,000 worth of notes. Assume that your depreciated basis is $120,000, but the value of the apartment building you get is $200,000. Then

Value of apartment house you received	$200,000	
Cash	20,000	
Notes	80,000	$300,000
Less: Value of apartment transferred by you		120,000
Gain on the exchange		$180,000
Boot received:		
Cash	$ 20,000	
Notes	80,000	
Gain recognized to extent of boot		$100,000
Gain postponed		$ 80,000

How are gains and losses on options taxed?

An option is a contract to keep an offer open. Suppose you have an option to purchase a piece of commercial real estate. Assume that you've paid the seller $1,000 for the option. Several situations can arise:

You fail to exercise the option. The $1,000 constitutes ordinary income to the seller regardless of the length of time that the offer is open. The reason is that an option is considered to have been "sold" on the day it expires; consequently the question of a long-term capital gain doesn't enter the picture.

You exercise the option. Again the $1,000 is ordinary income to the seller. You, however, add the $1,000 to the cost of the property. The new cost figure is taken into account when you sell the property.

The property appreciates in value, you sell the option for a profit, and your buyer exercises the option. Because the option is for a parcel of commercial property, it is a capital asset; if you've held onto it in excess of six months, you are entitled to a long-term capital gain.

In the case of a personal residence the situation changes. Suppose you have an option, again for $1,000, to buy a personal residence. The property goes down in value, and you decide not to exercise the option. You lose the $1,000 that you've paid for it. This loss is *not* deductible because loss on the sale of a personal residence is not deductible.

Warning: Generally the delivery of possession under an option without transfer of title does not constitute a taxable deduction. The problem arises like so: Suppose Mrs. Smith has just purchased a property for $20,000. She has an opportunity a few days later to sell it for $30,000. She wants to avoid the short-term tax on the $10,000 profit, and so goes to a buyer and arranges for the buyer to take an option on the property. The deal is that the buyer is to have immediate possession and then after six months exercise the option. Mrs. Smith figures that in this way she can switch the $10,000 profit from ordinary income to a long-term capital gain—so she thinks.

It's a pretty good bet that the IRS will look askance at this plan. It will argue that the sale actually took place when the option was executed (signed) and *not* at the subsequent date when the option was exercised.

re there tax-deductible depreciations in leases?

Generally not, but some people have tried. Suppose, for example, that Harry and Jane get together and decide that they are really going to beat Uncle Sam the Tax Man. Harry agrees to lease a property to Jane for 10 years at, say, $1,000 per year, and gives Jane an option to buy the property at that time. Harry says that he can depreciate the property during that time because he will be the owner of rental property and thus be home free on the $1,000 per year that he will be receiving as "rent." Jane figures that this will be great because during that time she can deduct the $1,000 per year as an expense and she, too, will be home free.

There's *no way* that this can be done. The IRS will look behind the "lease" and try to determine the intent of the parties. The "lease" will be construed as a "sale" and not as a lease and will be so treated for tax purposes. In addition, there's a good chance of penalties and fines.

How are security deposits on leases taxed?

It depends a great deal on how they are handled. Some states require that security deposits not be comingled with the funds of the landlord. In these states the tax problem does not arise unless the deposit is forfeited. In the case of a forfeiture, the deposit would be taxable as ordinary income at the time that the right of the landlord to the money was fixed and determined.

In a number of states landlords can, for all practical purposes, do with the deposits pretty much as they wish. If they choose to put them in a separate account and not use the funds, then the deposits are treated as outlined above. However, if the landlord uses the money, the deposit is labeled *advance rent* and, at the time when used, is taxable as ordinary income.

Suppose somebody leaves another person property in a will?

The question here really is, "What is the basis or value of the property for tax purposes?" It is the value of the property at the death of the decedent or the alternative valuation. The *alternative valuation* means the value of the property at the date of disposition of the property by the beneficiary or six months from the date of death, whichever occurs first.

Suppose you are left a piece of property by an uncle who paid $20,000 for it 10 years ago. At the time of his death, it is worth $30,000. You keep it for two years and sell it for $40,000. The tax is applicable on $10,000. ($40,000 selling price − $30,000 value at date of death = $10,000.)

What are the special rules applying to hobby farms?

In the past many people have purchased what have been labeled *hobby* farms. The object of the game is to buy the farm, take tremendous write-offs, wait for the land to appreciate in value, sell it, then take your long-term capital gains treatment.

But after 1969 special rules were adopted for high-income-bracket taxpayers not primarily engaged in farming. Basically, *losses* may be recaptured as ordinary income when property is sold or exchanged. The rule applies if a taxpayer has an adjusted gross income of $50,000 or over. But only to farm losses that exceed $25,000. In these cases an excess "deductions" account must be kept. Each year's net farm loss is added, and each year's net income is deducted. For example,

Year	Losses		Income		
1	$28,000		$2,000		
2	$12,000		$6,000		
	$40,000	minus	$8,000	=	$32,000 loss

Assume then that the property is sold. The excess deduction amounts to $7,000. ($32,000 loss − $25,000 allowed = $7,000.)

11 / DECISION

A wise man once remarked that in any decision-making process there are two steps—first, you decide to decide; second, you decide.

You might want to begin by asking yourself the question, "What kind of investor do I want to be?" In short, "What are my objectives or combination of objectives?" Am I

1 *An Investor for Use?* Here the investment is primarily in a home or residential condominium with its hedge against inflation, its interest deductions, and its real property tax deduction. Or the investment for use may be in a business building with depreciation constituting an additional tax advantage. Furthermore, over time you'll be building up equity with an investment in a business building.

2 *An Investor for Income?* The investment here is in property ranging from single-tenant realty to the apartment house or other income-producing property. You are buying a future stream of income, a hedge against inflation, and a tax shelter.

3 *An Investor for Appreciation?* This type of investment consists mainly of vacant land or farms and ranches. Frequently, however, other real property investments produce gains through appreciation. The investor here makes out because of possible long-term capital gains tax advantages and interest and property tax deductions.

4 *A Lender-Investor?* These investors are the straight mortgage investors, the purchasers of tax certificates, as well as the discount buyers of second mortgages and contracts. Earnings come principally from interest, but there is no inflation hedge or tax shelter.

How to get money

Money for real estate investment can be made available by shifting the form of savings assets, for example, moving cash out of a savings and loan account to real property. Obviously financing is easier for persons having large amounts of savings, but opportunities exist for persons with limited means.

Do look at the loan value of your life insurance policies. True, the companies are paying you interest on these savings, but the rate that you receive is about 4.8 percent, which means that, in times of double-digit inflation, you are losing between 6 and 7 percent a year.

Do reexamine liquid savings held in such institutions as savings and loan associations or mutual savings banks. Despite their advertisements, letting them hold your money results in your losing purchasing power by reason of inflation. Think in terms of the amount of ready cash you need. Take the amount you have in your savings account which is above your immediate cash needs and invest it in real estate.

Do reexamine any monies you have invested in the stock market. At one time it was thought that common stock was a hedge against inflation. Recent studies suggest that this is no longer so. Think, too, of the fact that stocks provide no tax shelter—except when there are losses.

Do, if your capital is relatively small, think of a small syndicate consisting of your friends and family. Together you can chip in on an investment in real property. Many people do this.

Do contact Realtors. They are professionals. Have them look for attractive investments. Sometimes they are aware of opportunities for investment with relatively small down payments.

And remember the old saying: The person who doesn't take a chance can never win.

Index